WESTMAR COLLEGE

W9-CDU-227

BEN JONSON
AND
ELIZABETHAN MUSIC

Da Capo Press Music Titles

FREDERICK FREEDMAN, General Editor

University of California at Los Angeles

BEN JONSON

AND

ELIZABETHAN MUSIC

Willa McClung Evans

With a new Preface to the Second Printing

Da Capo Press
New York
1965

781.96
J66Ze

ML
80
.J7
E8
1965

A
Da Capo Press
Reprint Edition

First Da Capo Printing – August 1965
Second Da Capo Printing – March 1967

This edition is an unabridged reprint
of the first edition published in 1929
by Lancaster Press.

Library of Congress Catalog Card No. 65-18503

© *1965 Da Capo Press*
A Division of Consultants Bureau Enterprises, Inc.
227 West 17th Street • New York, N. Y. 10011

Printed in the United States of America

82615

PREFACE TO A SECOND PRINTING

No book, obviously, provides the final appraisal of a great poet's accomplishment. This study does not pretend to relate all that might be said of Jonson's construction of stanzas for musical settings or of his dramatic uses of song. My original project was the exploration of what was, in the 1920's, a new and limited field for literary search. Since the first printing of this monograph in 1929, a variety of studies have broadened the scope for such exploration. While it is futile to attempt in a preface to refer to all of the titles that should be included in a supplement to the original bibliography on pages 122–131, I shall point in these paragraphs to several studies which have enriched the field of *Ben Jonson and Elizabethan Music,* thereby converting it into a subject for profitable future investigation.

Basic to further quest is the completion of an eleven-volume edition of *Ben Jonson* edited by Herford and the Simpsons.[1] Of special interest is the list of "Musical Settings of Jonson's Songs," which appears in the eleventh volume, page 605. By no means basic, but of interest, are the biographies of Jonson intended for popular consumption.[2] Their appearance testifies to the vigorous appeal which their subject still possesses, reflecting to a degree the exuberance of a nature for which the expression of song was an aesthetic compulsion. Reverting to the scholarly commentary on Jonson that has flowed since 1929, I should call attention first to Knight's *Drama and Society in the Age of Jonson.*[3] Though not slanted to show that Jonson absorbed and reflected the song of

[1] *Ben Jonson,* ed. by C. H. Herford, Percy and Evelyn Simpson, 11 vols. (Oxford: Clarendon Press, 1925–52).

[2] Marchette Chute, *Ben Jonson of Westminster* (New York: E. P. Dutton, 1953); Eric Linklater, *Ben Jonson and King James; Biography and Portrait* (London: Jonathan Cape, 1931); John Leslie Palmer, *Ben Jonson* (London: George Routledge & Sons; New York: Viking Press, 1934); Byron Steel [pseud. of Francis Steegmüller], *O Rare Ben Jonson* (New York: A. A. Knopf, 1927).

[3] L. C. Knight, *Drama and Society in the Age of Jonson* (London: Chatto & Windus, 1937).

his time, it provides a process of persuasion which might well be applied in explaining the playwright's reactions to music. In *Ben Jonson: Poet*,[4] George Burke Johnston indicated that Jonson's poetic techniques were at least in part developed from his reactions to contemporary song. Later in this preface, I shall have occasion to refer to commentary of Jonson's uses of symbols and his dependency upon classical models. Without making a further attempt to point to specific studies of Jonson here, I shall simply call attention to the important, yet selected, bibliography in William B. Hunter's edition of Ben Jonson's *Complete Poetry*[5] and to *Ben Jonson*, edited by Jonas A. Barish.[6]

In another category there are several books which, while they do not focus upon Jonson himself nor on his life and works, employ analytical discussions of his uses of music. Some of these have for their purpose the demonstration of the overall relationship between Elizabethan music and poetry. In 1940, Boyd surveyed this field in his *Elizabethan Music and Musical Criticism*.[7] Several years later, Bruce Pattison extended its boundaries with his *Music and Poetry of the English Renaissance*.[8] And as recently as 1962, Gretchen Finney, in a series of articles collectively issued as *Musical Backgrounds for English Literature: 1580–1650*,[9] stressed the significance of music as contributory to poetic composition — particularly Milton's.

Outstanding among the works treating of Jonson's colleagues among the playwrights, studies which draw upon his uses of music as being illustrative of contemporary practices in dramaturgy are John Long's two-volume study of Shakespeare and music entitled *Shakespeare's Use of Music*[10] and *Music in Shakespearean*

[4] George Burke Johnston, *Ben Jonson: Poet* (New York: Columbia University Press, 1945).

[5] Ben Jonson, *Complete Poetry*, ed. by William B. Hunter (New York: New York University Press, 1963).

[6] Jonas A. Barish, ed., *Ben Jonson, A Collection of Critical Essays* (Englewood Cliffs, N. J.: Prentice-Hall, 1963).

[7] Morrison Comegys Boyd, *Elizabethan Music and Musical Criticism* (Philadelphia: University of Pennsylvania Press, 1940); 2nd ed., 1962.

[8] Bruce Pattison, *Music and Poetry of the English Renaissance* (London: Methuen, 1948).

[9] Gretchen Ludke Finney, *Musical Backgrounds for English Literature: 1580–1650* (New Brunswick: Rutgers University Press, 1962).

[10] John H. Long, *Shakespeare's Use of Music*, 2 vols. (Gainesville: University of Florida Press, 1955–1961). [Vol. I: *A Study of the Music and Its Performance in the Original Production of Seven Comedies*; Vol. II: *The Final Comedies*.]

Tragedy.[11] Joan Webber's *Contrary Music: The Prose Style of John Donne*[12] does not, properly speaking, belong to this category but should be mentioned because the method of analysis employed might be paralleled at some points in future treatments of Jonson's verse. Among the numerous articles on nondramatic contemporary verse and music, Alicia Ostriker's "Song and Speech in the Metrics of George Herbert"[13] takes on importance because of its fresh approach.

Perhaps the most impressive category of studies contributing to the scope of *Ben Jonson and Elizabethan Music* is that treating of the nature of song itself. Musicologists have been extraordinarily active. A general guide such as Vincent Duckles' *Music Reference and Research Materials*[14] leads us to locate important reference and research tools, some items of which even locate source material for future search. But there are more particular directives available in E. F. Hart's "Caroline Lyrics and Contemporary Song-books,"[15] Margaret Crum's "A Manuscript of John Wilson's Songs,"[16] and Duckles' "The Gamble Manuscript as a Source of Continuo Song in England."[17] Recent editions of music manuscripts and early printed books have made material concerning Jonson's associates more accessible. The facsimile edition of John Coperario's *Rules How to Compose*,[18] with an introduction by Manfred Bukofzer, contributes valuable commentary on one

[11] Frederick W. Sternfeld, *Music in Shakespearean Tragedy* (London: Routledge & Kegan Paul; New York: Dover, 1963).

[12] Joan Webber, *Contrary Music: The Prose Style of John Donne* (Madison: University of Wisconsin Press, 1963).

[13] Alicia Ostriker, "Song and Speech in the Metrics of George Herbert," *Publications of the Modern Language Association of America* LXXX/1 (March 1965), 62–68.

[14] Vincent H. Duckles, *Music Reference and Research Materials: An Annotated Bibliography* (New York: The Free Press of Glencoe; London: Collier-Macmillan Limited, 1964).

[15] E. F. Hart, "Caroline Lyrics and Contemporary Song-books," *The Library: A Quarterly Review of Bibliography*, 5th Series, VIII/2 (June 1953), 89–110.

[16] Margaret Crum, "A Manuscript of John Wilson's Songs," *ibid.*, 5th Series, X/1 (March 1955), 55–57.

[17] Vincent H. Duckles, "The Gamble Manuscript as a Source of Continuo Song in England," *Journal of the American Musicological Society* I/2 (Summer 1948), 23–40. [Duckles' unpublished doctoral dissertation, University of California at Berkeley, 1953, may also be of interest: "John Gamble's *Commonplace Book*: A Critical Edition of New York Public Library MS Drexel 4257."]

[18] John Coperario, *Rules How to Compose*, with an introduction by Manfred Bukofzer (Los Angeles: Ernest E. Gottlieb, 1952).

of Jonson's collaborators. Modern editions of Thomas Morley's works, such as his treatise entitled *A Plain and Easy Introduction to Practical Music*[19] and Sydney Beck's edition of *The First Book of Consort Lessons, Collected by Thomas Morley,*[20] provide illuminative information concerning another of Jonson's associates.

Two full-length biographies of musicians contribute additional facts concerning Jonson's connection with the composers. Murray Lefkowitz[21] considers the relationship between William Lawes and Jonson puzzling but points (see pages 16, 279) to a musical setting for "A Dialogue between the Passions" and alludes to the poet in a dozen other passages. My own study of *Henry Lawes, Musician and Friend of Poets*[22] prints in facsimile a setting for one of Jonson's lyrics, and in some seventeen references calls attention to facets of his activities relative to Henry Lawes that came to my attention after 1929. In an article on Alphonso Ferrabosco, A. J. Renwick[23] contributes further information concerning another of Jonson's collaborators.

By no means the least significant of the categories of studies amplifying the scope of my original project are those which have been made of the court masque and music of the theater. Among the former, Otto Gombosi's "Some Musical Aspects of the English Court Masque"[24] is most pertinent to my Chapter III; among the latter, Manifold's "Theatre Music in the Sixteenth and Seventeenth Centuries"[25] and *The Music in English Drama, from Shakespeare to Purcell*[26] are most pertinent to my Chapter II.

The most important contribution that has been made to the

[19] Thomas Morley, *A Plain and Easy Introduction to Practical Music,* ed. by R. Alec Harman with a foreword by Thurston Dart (London: J. M. Dent & Sons, Ltd., 1952) [reprinted, 1963].

[20] Sydney Beck, ed., *The First Book of Consort Lessons, Collected by Thomas Morley, 1599 & 1611* (New York: C. F. Peters for The New York Public Library, 1959).

[21] Murray Lefkowitz, *William Lawes* (London: Routledge & Kegan Paul; New York: Dover, 1960).

[22] Willa McClung Evans, *Henry Lawes, Musician and Friend of Poets* (New York: Modern Language Association, 1941).

[23] A. J. Renwick, "Alphonso Ferrabosco," *The Review of English Studies* XI [No. 42] (April 1935), 184–185.

[24] Otto Gombosi, "Some Musical Aspects of the English Court Masque," *Journal of the American Musicological Society* I/3 (Fall 1948), 3–19.

[25] John S. Manifold, "Theatre Music in the Sixteenth and Seventeenth Centuries," *Music and Letters* XXIX/4 (October 1948), 366–397.

[26] _____, *The Music in English Drama, from Shakespeare to Purcell* (London: Rockliff, 1956).

project described as *Ben Jonson and Elizabethan Music* has been the discovery of additional settings for Jonson's lyrics. Several are reported in the studies cited above. Other writings of considerable interest include three articles by John Cutts, "Original Music to Browne's *Inner Temple Masque,* and Other Jacobean Masque Music,"[27] "Volpone's Song,"[28] and "Robert Johnson and the Court Masque"[29]; Emslie's "Nicholas Lanier's Innovations in English Song"[30]; Andrew J. Sabol's "A Newly Discovered Contemporary Song Setting for Jonson's 'Cynthia's Revels',"[31] and "Two Unpublished Stage Songs for the *Aery of Children* "[32] and Frederick W. Sternfeld's "Song in Jonson's Comedy: A Gloss on *Volpone.*"[33]

During the years of expansion and extension of my subject, some of my observations have been confirmed, some have been questioned. Since a preface is not the appropriate place in which to take notice of the former or to refute the latter, I shall not identify by title either kind of commentary. Nor shall I fully express my contrition for the inadequacies of an immature style all too abundantly evidenced on these pages.

Admitting, then, the book's limitations, I propose to offer here reasons for reprinting it. In the first place, this dissertation provides commentary upon fashions in academic exercises. The project was a departure from what was considered in the 1920's appropriate for a Ph.D. enterprise: the probing of literary sources. Because *Ben Jonson and Elizabethan Music* involved a demonstration of the relationship between two arts, an association then

[27] John P. Cutts, "Original Music to Browne's *Inner Temple Masque,* and Other Jacobean Masque Music," *Notes and Queries* 199 [New Series I/5] (May 1954), 194–195.

[28] _____, "Volpone's Song. A Note on the Source and Jonson's Translation," *Notes and Queries* 203 [New Series V/5] (May 1958), 217–219.

[29] _____,"Robert Johnson and the Court Masque," *Music and Letters* XLI/2 (April 1960), 111–126.

[30] McDonald Emslie, "Nicholas Lanier's Innovations in English Song," *Music and Letters* XLI/1 (January 1960), 13–27.

[31] Andrew J. Sabol, "A Newly Discovered Contemporary Song Setting for Jonson's 'Cynthia's Revels'," *Notes and Queries* 203 [New Series V/9] (September 1958), 384–385.

[32] _____, "Two Unpublished Stage Songs for the *Aery of Children,*" *Renaissance News* VIII/3 (Autumn 1960), 222-232.

[33] Frederick W. Sternfeld, "Song in Jonson's Comedy: A Gloss on *Volpone,*" in *Studies in the English Renaissance Drama,* ed. by Josephine W. Bennett, Oscar Cargill, and Vernon Hall, Jr. (New York: New York University Press, 1959), 310–321.

held somewhat suspect, to obtain permission to undertake the task was difficult. Though it was conceded that Milton and Campion have been influenced by music, it had long been assumed that Jonson had learned his techniques as poet and playwright solely from classical models.[34] One critic from whom I sought advice assured me that in the sixteenth and seventeenth centuries there had been no alliance between music and poetry; another pointed out that he had himself contributed all that ought to be said on the subject. Because of such counsel, I concentrated my efforts on establishing the soundness of my theories, thereby failing to stress sufficiently the manner of setting them forth. (To those kindly, brave, and indulgent advisers who encouraged me, I attempted in the first printing of this book to express my gratitude.) I call attention here to early difficulties since it is hard to realize that what is now taken for granted was once exploration.

One further comment should be made upon trends in academic exercise as demonstrated in this monograph. The absorption in symbolism, which developed after I had finished my study, came too late to affect the content of these pages. More important, however, is the fact that, so far as I am aware, a full-length treatment of Jonson's uses of music as symbol has yet to be written.[35]

[34] The pendulum of fashion in academic studies may have swung back to its 1920 position. In 1951, Catherine M. Ing, *Elizabethan Lyrics: A Study in the Development of English Metres and Their Relation to Poetic Effect* (London: Chatto & Windus, 1951), attempted to define the characteristics of Jonson's two debts, one to classical models, the other to contemporary song patterns. In view of her well-slanted beginning, it is surprising that Wesley Trimpi, in *Ben Jonson's Poems: A Study of the Plain Style* (Stanford: Stanford University Press, 1962), paid scant attention to Jonson's uses of music. Except for an occasional brief allusion (as on p. 233) to the "metrical conventions of the Elizabethan songbooks and to the popular ballad meters," Trimpi attributes the power of Jonsons poems to classical influences.

[35] Allan H. Gilbert, *The Symbolic Persons in the Masques of Ben Jonson* (Durham: Duke University Press, 1948), and Ernest William Talbert, "The Interpretation of Jonson's Courtly Spectacles," *Publications of the Modern Language Association of America* LXI/2 (June 1946), 454–473, have opened the way for such a study. John Hollander, *The Untuning of the Sky; Ideas of Music in English Poetry, 1500–1700* (Princeton: Princeton University Press, 1961), alludes to Jonson's symbols in establishing the validity of a new critique (see index under *Jonson*). Ray L. Heffner, Jr., "Unifying Symbols in the Comedy of Ben Jonson," *English Institute Essays: 1954* (New York: Columbia University Press, 1955), 74–97, analyzes several Jonsonian symbols pertinent to music. This article was reprinted in *Ben Jonson, A Collection of Critical Essays*, edited by Barish, n. 6.

The main reason for permitting the reprinting of this dissertation is that I am still convinced that the overall thesis is sound. Jonson's rise and decline as lyricist and playwright were paralleled by the degree of his intimacy and collaboration with musicians. The greater the demand for stanzas to be sung on the public stage and at the court, the more numerous and the better were the lyrics Jonson provided. Composers invited and encouraged the expansion of his abilities. But when the poet became old, sick, disillusioned with the court, and saw less and less of palace life and of the King's musicians,[36] there was little impetus for him to write songs. His lyricism, when manifest, became reminiscent of an earlier age of music rather than responsive to the standards set for immediate or future performance. During these later years, Jonson's technical control over his poetic control may not have diminished; but his absence from the society and requirements of composers was certainly among the causes resulting in the lapse from and eventual eclipse of his exercise of lyrical power.

A final reason for reprinting this book is that today, when it is reported that projects for research in the liberal arts are largely exhausted,[37] the very inadequacies of my study — by challenging efforts to improve upon them — offer many new subjects for investigation. Let future explorers in this field complete the survey here begun. Let them establish how much still needs to be turned over and brought to light. Let them be less dogmatic than my successors and I have been; but let them draw a finer line than we between the structural patterns Jonson borrowed from classical song and those he adopted from contemporary composers, and between stanzas designed for late sixteenth-century polyphonic settings and those for early seventeenth-century recitative and ayre arrangements. Let future students distinguish between

[36] Jonson's relationship to the King's musicians has never been fully examined. Foundations for such investigation have been laid in such works as *King's Music: An Anthology*, by Gerald R. Hayes, with an essay by Sir H. Walford Davies (London: Oxford University Press, 1937); Walter L. Woodfill, *Musicians in English Society from Elizabeth to Charles I* (Princeton: Princeton University Press, 1953); and Gerald E. Aylmer, *The King's Servants; the Civil Service of Charles I, 1625–1642* (New York: Columbia University Press, 1961).

[37] Morris Bishop in his presidential address before the Modern Language Association, "Research and Reward," *Publications of the Modern Language Association of America* LXXX/1 (March 1965), 3–8, considers the subject matter for academic research largely exhausted and discusses at some length "how to fit an excess of skilled workers to a paucity of work to be done."

Jonson's reflection and his *shaping* of the fashion for noblemen to perform music in public. Let those who quest for hidden meanings explain how through direct references to and figures of speech based on music, and through stanzaic structure and dramatic devices, Jonson created symbols that express truth and comment upon the world and those that dwell therein.

For those who are looking for literary and/or musicological problems to solve, particularly for those who can penetrate what yet remains to be done — and are willing to begin where my successors and I have left off — this book is now reprinted.

WILLA McCLUNG EVANS

BEN JONSON
AND
ELIZABETHAN MUSIC

Ome my *Ce-li-a*, let vs proue, while wee may the sweets of

loue, Time wil not be ours for euer, he at length our good wil se- uer, Spend not then his gifts in

vaine, Sunnes that set may rise a- gain, But if we once loose this light, tis with vs perpe-

tuall night, Why should wee deferre our ioyes, fame and rumour are but toyes? Cannot

we delude the eyes of a few poore houshold spyes, Or his easier eares beguile, Thus remoued by our

wile T'is no ſinne loues fruits to ſteale, But the ſweet theft to re- ueale, To be taken, to be ſeene,

Theſe haue crimes ac- counted been.to be taken,to be ſeene,Theſe haue crimes ac- counted beene,

VI.

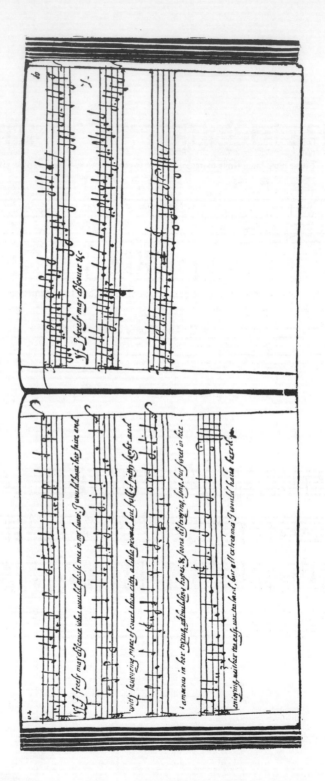

BEN JONSON AND ELIZABETHAN MUSIC

By

WILLA McCLUNG EVANS

LANCASTER, PENNSYLVANIA
LANCASTER PRESS, INC.

1929

Copyright, 1929
by
WILLA M. EVANS

To My Father
And to the Memory of My Mother

CONTENTS

Thanks are due to the English faculty of Columbia University for helpful suggestions and criticisms during the preparation of this dissertation, particularly to Dr. H. W. Wells, whose interest in the subject encouraged me to undertake the study. I am glad to have an opportunity to acknowledge my indebtedness to Professor H. M. Ayres for assistance in shaping and clarifying the problem. To Professor A. H. Thorndike I am especially grateful. Without his long-continued stimulation, kindly criticisms, and guidance in the organization of my material, this study would have been impossible.

INTRODUCTION

"'Tis a singing age, Sir, . . ."
—John Fletcher, *The Loyal Subject,* II. 1

The London of Ben Jonson's age was vibrant with lute and viol, part-song and madrigal. Enthusiasm for music was so much a part of Elizabethan life that even "tinkers sang catches; milkmaids, ballads; carters whistled; and the beggars had their special songs."[1] "There was music at dinner, music at supper, music at work, and music at play."[2] Henry Peacham demanded that every man who would be called a gentleman should learn to "sing his part sure and at first sight, withall."[3] Thomas Morley relates a story about a sad young man whose social career was temporarily blighted because he could not join his hostess in an after-dinner madrigal.[4] Falstaff had, on occasion, lost his voice "hallelujahing and singing of anthems."[5] The spirit of song was indeed riotous when all the world was singing psalms to hornpipes. Quite naturally, the poets responded to the demands for songs by writing verses for music.

Into this singing world came Ben Jonson, who was a keen observer of all that went on about him. He was undoubtedly aware of the musical interests, enthusiasms, and outbursts of his companions. Today he is remembered primarily for his scholarly achievements; sometimes we forget he was a frequenter of taverns. Even though he was a man of pedantic temperament, his scholarly pursuits need not have prevented him from hearing insinuating melodies. His studious midnight quiet may possibly have been broken in upon by a certain Puritan parson who "sat up late of nights, singing catches."[6] Whatever the poet's tastes, whatever his habits and talents, the musical forces of the age could hardly fail to affect him.

[1] Chappell, William, *Popular Music of the Olden Time,* Volume I, p. 98.
[2] *Ibid.,* Volume I, p. 98.
[3] *The Compleat Gentleman,* London, 1622, Chapter XI. Reprinted with an Introduction by G. S. Gordon, Clarendon Press, 1906, p. 100.
[4] *A Plaine and Easie Introduction to Practickall Musicke,* 1597, p. 1.
[5] *2 Henry* IV, II, 2.
[6] *Epicœne,* III, 2.

Jonson's formal musical education began at Westminster College, where the students took part daily in the music of divine service.[7] After the school years had passed, and the young playwright began to study public demands, theater audiences were shouting for tunes.[8] Strains of part-songs, rounds, catches, and ballads sounded along the streets of London. Fiddlers swarmed at the taverns; the Mermaid certainly attracted its share of musicians. Motets, canzonets and madrigals floated along the corridors of Whitehall. Ladies-in-waiting and grooms-of-the-chamber displayed their talents in the court masque. It was inevitable that Jonson should note and record evidences of Elizabethan fondness for song. Accordingly we find his plays abounding in allusions to music.

In *Bartholomew Fair,* young Cokes is worrying his tutor by " learning of vile tunes which he will sing at supper, and in the sermon times." [9] This same Cokes, had, as a child, plastered the chimney corner of his nursery with ballads.[10]

Balladry was the occasion of many of Jonson's comments upon music. There was a ballad man standing on a London corner who could reel off " forty yards of ballad more." [11] Nightingale, the ballad seller in Bartholomew Fair, was an exceptionally clever musical scoundrel who transported his audience with enthralling melodies, while Cut-purse, an accomplice, robbed the listeners of their gold without awakening suspicion.[12] Also there was Nano, whose street singing invited so many customers to Volpone's shop

[7] Walcott, M. E. C. *Memorials of Westminster College,* London, 1869, p. 189. Also see *Curriculum.*

[8] " There is evidence that patrons of the drama used to cry out between the acts for tunes they fancied . . .", G. H. Cowling, *Music on the Shakespearean Stage,* Cambridge Univ. Press, 1913, p. 68. See also the close of Act II of *The Knight of the Burning Pestle,* when the Citizen calls out: " You musicians, play Baloo " (the name of a tune). " No, good George, let's ha' Lachrymae," entreats his wife, etc. Sir Bulstrode Whitelock's *Memorials* recount that Whitelock's Coranto, which was often played at the Blackfriar's, was " often called for." Quoted in Burney's *History of Music,* Volume III, p. 376.

[9] I, 1.

[10] III, 1.

[11] *Pleasure Reconciled to Virtue, Ben Jonson's Masques and Entertainments,* edited by Henry Morley, London, 1890, p. 223. References to the masques unless otherwise noted are based upon this edition, because this collection is perhaps more convenient for reference than any other.

[12] *Bartholomew Fair,* III, 1.

that the building had to be barricaded against invading crowds.[13]

Jonson refers to musical barbers,[14] singing tinkers,[15] tuneful augurers,[16] and lutenist printers.[17] But of all the singing world, the Jonsonian Beau Brummel was the most ridiculous as well as the most obviously devoted to music. "He doth . . . keep a barber, and a monkey; he has a rich . . . waistcoat. . . . He loves to have a . . . pedant, and a musician seen in his lodgings a-mornings."[18] He could "melt away his time, and never feel it! What between his . . . high fare, soft lodging, fine clothes, and his *fiddle,* he thinks the hours have no wings, or the day no post-horse."[19] His last words before slumber were apt to be: "I may go sleep 'till the revelling music wake me."[20] A set of violins was a desirable part of the equipment of a young man of fashion. Having ascertained this fact, and desiring to acquire the ear-marks of a man of the world, Cokes approached a booth at Bartholomew Fair, exclaiming: "A set of these violins I would buy too, for a delicate young noise I have in the country, that are every one of a size less than another, just like your fiddles. I would fain have a fine young masque at my marriage."[21] A young blood who knew no music might as well "make some desperate way"[22] with himself. Fastidious Brisk hoped to enhance the charm of his conversation with Saviolina by thrumming on the viol-de-gamba.[23] When Deliro attempted to appease his angry wife, he took home a bevy of fiddlers to help him sue for peace.[24] Elizabethan gallants believed the feminine heart was peculiarly subject to the softening influences of melody. Even the Puritan Parson felt that a "tune might do much with women."[25] Lady Politick-Would-Be herself justified their belief by boasting that she was "all for music."[26]

[13] *Volpone,* II, 1.
[14] *Vision of Delight, op. cit.,* p. 217.
[15] *Pan's Anniversary, ibid.,* p. 334.
[16] *Masque of Augurs, ibid.,* p. 299.
[17] *News from the New World,* p. 244.
[18] *Cynthia's Revels,* II, 1.
[19] *Epicœne,* I, 1.
[20] *Cynthia's Revels,* IV, 1.
[21] *Bartholomew Fair,* III, 1.
[22] *Cynthia's Revels,* IV, 1.
[23] *E. M. O.,* III, 3.
[24] *Ibid.*
[25] *The Alchemist,* III, 2.
[26] *Volpone,* III, 2.

Wherever merry gentlemen gathered round a festal board there was the rousing cheer of "drum gentlemen and trumpeters."[27] The flowing bowl and venison pasty attracted troops of musicians. The very smell of venison going through the streets "invited one noise of fiddlers or another."[28]   The trumpeters "had intelligence of all the feasts."[29]   There was a "good correspondence between them and the London cooks."[30]   Important dishes were pompously carried in to the blast of a trumpet; even "lesser viands" were "preceded to the table by the sound of music."[31]   The din of drum and trumpet rivalled hilarious shouting as the guests drank the King's health.

In his ramblings through Theocritus, Jonson found allusions to a kind of music he had never heard at the Mermaid, or the Boar's Head.   He came upon descriptions of evil incantations, which he copied laboriously with the hope that similar effects could be produced in the *Masque of Queens*.[32]   Everywhere he sought for suggestions of infernal harmony to furnish his witch-hags with appropriately satanic revels.   During the process of his searching, the poet collected enough odd facts, obscure details, and amusing anecdotes to make a history of primitive and classic song.   Time and again, he refers to the music of the spheres,[33] to Pythagoras' theories,[34] and Plato's doctrines.[35]

Yet another aspect of music associated with classic traditions, and one which was of immediate importance to the masques, was the song-lore of the ancient Greeks.   Olympian gods and goddesses were, like Jonson's friends and neighbors, absorbed by melody.   In the *Poetaster*, weary deities cry for music to stimulate their fatigued spirits.[36]   In the masques, wild Satyrs sport with the pipes of Pan.[37]   Apollo descends from high heaven tun-

[27] *Epicœne*, III, 1.
[28] *Ibid.*
[29] *Ibid.*
[30] *Ibid.*
[31] *Ibid.*
[32] *Masque of Queens, op. cit.,* footnote p. 105.
[33] *Cynthia's Revels,* I, 1.
[34] *Volpone,* III, 2.
[35] *Ibid.*
[36] *Poetaster,* IV, 3.
[37] *The Satyr, op. cit.,* p. 408.

ing his conch shell lyre; [38] echoes of Harmony's rending chords tremble across the lute strings.[39]

In fact, Jonson's Olympians seldom appeared in public unaccompanied by music. Song enhanced the emotional effect of their entrances and exits.[40] It helped to increase the illusion of their divinity. Not only did music emphasize their god-hood, but it interpreted their characters, and the nature of their commissions to earth. For instance, the bouncing God Comus bursts across the stage with laughter and shouting, to a " strange music of wild instruments " [41]—an appropriate entrance for the God of Cheer. In *Chloridia,* the scene opens with a serene sky filled with transparent clouds, " in a part of the air, a bright cloud begins to break forth; and in it is sitting a plump boy representing mild Zephyrus." [42] The boy sings, " Come forth, come forth, the Gentle Spring," [43]—a song which emphasizes the idyllic atmosphere of the setting. The boy's treble voice, accompanied by the lute,[44] might well woo the spirit of spring.

Song not only introduced characters; it interpreted settings and heightened the emotional appeal of pageantry. In *Neptune's Triumph,* the island of Delos moves backward and forward while the Muses and the goddess of Harmony make music, and Apollo sings.[45] This moving backward and forward required an accompaniment of song, not only to deaden the noises of rumbling stage machinery necessary to the shifting of the island, but also to suggest allurement, enchantment, mystery—qualities which were indeed proper for the interpretation of such a setting. Music was similarly introduced at the close of *Chloridia,* when " Fame begins to mount, and moving her wings flieth singing up to Heaven." [46]

By far the most revealing evidence of the poet's dependence upon " a divine rapture of music," occurs in the *Entertainment*

[38] *Augurs,* p. 299.

[39] *Neptune's Triumph,* p. 327.

[40] G. H. Cowling, in *Music on the Shakespearean Stage, op. cit.,* Chapter I. discusses the value of music in the presentation of deities and supernatural beings on the stage.

[41] *Pleasure Reconciled,* p. 222.

[42] *Chloridia,* p. 368.

[43] *Chloridia,* p. 368.

[44] Solos were usually accompanied by lutes, see Chapter I, p. 16.

[45] *Neptune's Triumph,* p. 327.

[46] *Chloridia,* p. 373.

at Theobald's.[47] Genius, who had been struck dumb through his admiration of the Queen, cannot find suitable words to express his feeling. Rendered speechless by emotion, he implores music to express his awe and homage:

> " There might you read my faith, my thoughts—But, O,
> My joys, like waves, each other overcome,
> And gladness drowns where it begins to flow!
> Some greater Powers speak out, for mine are dumb!

At this was the place filled with a rare and choice Music, to which was heard the following SONG delivered by an excellent voice, and the burden maintained by the whole Quire."

In view of Jonson's singular reticence in praising architecture, or painting, or other art-forms,[48] this glowing tribute to music might lead us to believe that he regarded song as part of his own province.[49]

Doubtless King James, whose pleasure in hunting amounted to a vice, took great delight in hearing bugles, the winding of cornets, and the calls of wind instruments which resembled the hunting horn. Equally flattering was the constant reminder of the pomp due to Majesty, which Jonson emphasized by frequent flourishes of drums and trumpets. The poet sought the King's favor, too, by appealing to the Sovereign's love of erudition. We find many allusions to the music of classical mythology, to the early bonds between music and song, and to Chaucer's, Gower's, Lydgate's, and Spenser's tributes to the lyre.[50]

Mirth and music, albeit sometimes in cumbrous phrase, frolic hand in hand through the plays, touching up solemn situations with light and genial humor. Hermogenes's brave singing in Act II, Scene 1, of the *Poetaster* is an essential comic element of the play. The situation opens in a room of a palace, where a group of fashionable ladies and gallants are waiting for a banquet to be served. One of the number, Crispinus, politely urges Hermog-

[47] *Entertainment at Theobald's*, p. 431.

[48] For a discussion of Jonson's attitude toward architecture, painting, etc., see *Ben Jonson, the Man and His Work*, Herford and Simpson, Oxford University Press, 1925, Volume I, p. 436. See also the Index for references to *Inigo Jones*, and *architecture*.

[49] For a study of Jonson's conception of his own art, and his own medium of expression, see Miss Esther Dunn's volume, *Ben Jonson's Art*, Smith College, Northampton, Mass., 1925.

[50] *The Golden Age Restored, op. cit.*, p. 197.

enes to speed the time with a little music. Hermogenes promptly
but stormily insists that he cannot sing. But Crispinus presses
him until he admits that he *can* sing, but *will* not. Refusal follows
refusal! Eventually the coaxing of friends prevails and he ren-
ders the requested solo. Once started, he has no desire to stop.
He volunteers one song after another. The audience grows restless, weary, then rebellious. Each song inspires Hermogenes to
surpass himself and each song adds to the impatience of the agi-
tated companions. At length the feast is served much to the
discomfiture of Hermogenes, and much to the relief of the fatigued audience. The guests make their escape sighing and urg-
ing each other out of the room lest Hermogenes begin " yet another " before they can make an exit.[51]

In *Bartholomew Fair*, Jonson pokes fun at an amateur's attempts to imitate a professional musician. Poor Cokes is trying
to learn one of Nightingale's songs by rote. But the young man
gets little beyond the first phrase of his song, when Nightingale's
accomplice robs him of his purse. Yet the simple fellow continues to repeat Nightingale's lines time after time, with no improvement in vocal interpretation:

> Youth, youth, thou hadst better been starved by thy nurse
> Than live to be hanged for cutting a purse.[52]

In *Epicœne,* Clerimont wishes to infuriate Morose, whose tan-
trums at the sound of even a slight whisper contribute the humorous element of the play. Clerimont visits Morose, taking
with him a troop of musicians, at whose notes Morose flies into
a fit of violent passion.[53]

Jonson's description of Welsh fondness for music includes amusing touches: " 'Is, the goat-herd and his dog and his son and his
wife *makes musiques* to the goats as they come from the hills;
. . . the elderly goats are indifferently grave at first . . . and
tread only it the measures. . . . The Welse goat is an excellent
dancer by birth." [54] Musical allusions such as this frequently
lighten the monotony of Jonson's heavier rhetorical passages.

[51] *The Poetaster,* II, 1.
[52] *Bartholomew Fair,* III, 1.
[53] *Epicœne,* III, 2.
[54] *For the Honour of Wales, op. cit.,* p. 239. (My italics.)

Punning was another way to relate wit and music.[55]   But wit and humor were not the only element of Jonson's style to profit by the use of a musician's vocabulary.   Musical terms furnished the poet with many a neatly expressed allusion.   His clear-cut similes and metaphors differed substantially from Dekker's more enthusiastic eulogies,—enthusiastic raptures over the " sphery soul " of music which flew on " wings of air," " invisibly," " yet enjoyed." [56]   Though Jonson's figures of speech reveal but slight enthusiasm, they show a deep understanding of music, and a sound appreciation of its values.   He was too practical, too rational to " Command music with her silver tongue to charm soft lullabyes unto his soul." [57]   But his explanation of the fledgling courtier's situation is both clear-cut and accurate; the courtier was " one but newly entered, who knew but the ut-re-me-fa-la-sol-la of courtship." [58]   The nonchalance with which he refers to an *undersong*,[59] *running a division* on a given air [60] a *cadence*,[61] a *die-note*,[62] etc. indicates a first hand knowledge of a musician's problems.

We have now assembled sufficient evidence to show that the music which was loved and practiced by the Elizabethans was much in Jonson's thoughts, and his allusions, his vocabulary, his use of music in the masques, etc., were but the natural responses to the musical enthusiasms of his age.

Such response, however, was not limited to the evidences we have just examined.   He was a prolific song-writer, engaging in writing lyrics to be sung on the stage, at the court masques, and also lyrics which were to be read in the quiet of a library.   An

[55] " Musicians cannot be but healthful; for they live by good *aire*." *Mountebank's Masque*, Shakes. Soc. pub., Vols. 38, 39, 41, p. 121.   " Who would believe dull Madge so sharp a singer? " *Masque of the Twelve Months, ibid.*, p. 138.   (Authorship?)

[56] *Westward Ho*, from the *Works of Thomas Dekker*, London, 1873, Volume II, p. 333.

[57] Dekker, Thomas, *Old Fortunatus*, Vol. I, p. 139.

[58] *Cynthia's Revels*, II, 1.

[59] *The Gypsies Metamorphosed*, p. 289.

[60] *E.M.O.* III, 3.

[61] *Blackness*, p. 43.

[62] *Cynthia's Revels*, IV, 1.

analysis of these varying types of song reveals certain differences in the technical application of musical laws to verse-form.

The idea of pointing out the relationship between song and verse is by no means new. Among sixteenth century critics, Ronsard advanced the theory that words were of very little importance without music, and gave the following advice to his disciples: " Make your verses masculine and feminine as far as you can, so as to be more proper to music and the harmony of instruments in favor of which it seems poetry was born; for poetry without instruments or without the grace of a single or several is in no wise agreeable." [63]   Thomas Campion, the English composer-poet, stated in the preface to his *First Book of Ayrs,* that he had tried to " marry the words and the notes lovingly together." [64]   Thomas Morley in his book of advice to young musicians and composers urges that the notes should develop from the words—that the music should emphasize the meaning and the feeling of each syllable. [65]

What has modern criticism done to carry forward the contemporary views toward an evaluation of the poetry? We are familiar with the poetry, and much has been said about poetic forms; but we are not familiar with the tunes which Ronsard, Campion, and Morley regarded as essential both to the composition and interpretation of Elizabethan lyric verse. If we are, however, to come to a keener, a closer appreciation of Elizabethan lyrics, we must re-examine the song-books, and consider the interrelation of the two arts. Among modern critics who have realized the importance of this relationship, A. H. Bullen was one of the first to comment upon the fact that " In Elizabethan times music was married to immortal verse." [66]   Andrew Lang, also, noted that the " exquisite accord of music and words in this [the Elizabethan] lyric has been noted by all competent judges." [67]

More recently, Edward Bliss Reed observed that the " Elizabethan composers wrote their poetry for music which in many

---

[63] Ronsard, Francois, *Art Poetique,* translated by W. L. Renwick, *Edmund Spenser,* London, 1925, p. 110.

[64] Campion, Thomas, see the Preface to the *First Book of Ayrs.*

[65] Morley, Thomas, *A Plaine and Easie Introduction to Practickall Musicke,* London, 1597.

[66] Bullen, A. H., *More Lyrics from the Elizabethan Song-Books,* London, 1888, Preface, p. 19.

[67] Lang, Andrew, *Elizabethan Songs,* Boston, 1894.

respects has never been surpassed." [68]   And a year later, Sigmund Spaeth, author of Milton's *Knowledge of Music,* echoed the sentiment that the "importance of words in vocal music led to a close alliance with the sister art of poetry, an alliance which showed its effects in most of the work of the great musicians of the day." [69]

Working upon such slender evidences as the allusions which poets have made to music, or upon biographical data, or upon the knowledge afforded by a few song-books, modern critics have tried to point out a definite connection between the arts. They were handicapped in drawing tangible facts from their studies because students of literature were without much knowledge of Elizabethan music. And failing to come upon any definite facts pointing to the relationship of music and poetry, some of these critics concluded that there was no relationship between the arts.

Among others, even Sidney Lanier championed the opinion that music "having found its fullest expression in the purely instrumental symphony" and poetry "its fullest expression in the purely vocal tunes of the speaking voice," each art went on to its fullest development alone.[70]

Professor John Erskine echoed and expanded Lanier's theory [71] in a dissertation on the *Elizabethan Lyric.* His conclusion that "Verse when it attains great verbal melody parts company with music and can best be appreciated alone" [72] was based upon inadequate source material. Professor Erskine believed that the poems for the song-books were written "simply as poetry, and were intended to appeal to that art alone." Such a statement does not take into account the fact that a great mass of the songs have never been identified as to authorship. Without definite details about the authorship, and exact information as to their origin, it is impossible to divine that the songs were "written simply as poetry

[68] Reed, E. B., *English Lyric Poetry,* Yale Univ. Press, New Haven, 1912, p. 214.

[69] Spaeth, S. G., *Milton's Knowledge of Music,* Princeton, 1913, p. 11.

[70] Lanier, Sydney, *The Science of English Verse,* Chas. Scribner's Sons Co., New York, 1880, p. 264.

[71] Hepple advances Lanier's theory, differing however, in placing the date of the separation of the arts during Dryden's time. Norman Hepple, *Lyrical Forms in English Verse, Cambridge* Univ. Press, 1916.

[72] Erskine, John, *The Elizabethan Lyric,* Columbia Univ. Press, 1903, p. 243.

and intended to appeal to that art alone." Moreover, of the small number which have been identified as to authorship, many were written by the composers themselves, who apparently had no purpose for writing other than setting them to music. Byrd, Dowland, and Weelkes certainly intended the words which they not only wrote, but also set to music, to be sung. Consideration should also be given to the fact that many Elizabethan songs were written for plays. Shakespeare, Dekker, Fletcher and other playwrights made songs to be sung on the stage. Ben Jonson, Campion, Shirley and other masque writers intended the songs in their masques to be set to music, and to make their appeal in actual musical performance. After considering these various phases of the composition of Elizabethan songs, we may come to doubt that Elizabethan songs " were written simply as poetry, and were intended to appeal to that art alone."

Within the last ten or fifteen years, Dr. Edmund Horace Fellowes has published a series of studies, the result of a life work of research on the Elizabethan Song-Books. Dr. Fellowes has searched out and made available over nine hundred lost songs of England. He has not only discovered the manuscripts, and edited songs, but written copiously on the nature and theory of the art. Owing to this investigation, Elizabethan music has received a new interpretation, a new value. Dr. Fellowes's work has been brilliantly supplemented by the performances of the English Singers. Musicians have taken the initial steps in establishing a bond between music and poetry. Barclay Squire, Vaughn Williams, Frederick Bridges, and others have carried forward and inspired research.

Today, even the musicians have adopted the attitude that English song was indeed inspired by the sounds of the spoken word. They support the theory that the Elizabethan period presents a time when the "twin arts of music and poetry were happily blended, when Shakespeare and the great poets of his generation worked side by side with the composers in intimate friendship." " And the greatest of English poetry was written during Shakespeare's time, with the particular purpose of being set to music." [73]

[73] *Treasures from the Golden Age of English Music,* an anonymous publication sponsored by the English Singers, published by Wm. H. Wise and Co., 50 West 47th Street, New York City, 1928, p. 6.

Since the musicians have opened new path-ways, and taken the first steps to establish a relation between music and poetry, students of literature have an opportunity to examine and reconsider Elizabethan lyrics in the light of recent musical criticism. It is the purpose of this study to point out various phases of the relationship between music and poetry as shown in the songs of Ben Jonson. I have chosen the poetry of Ben Jonson because there is no doubt that he wrote many of his lyrics for singing. Moreover, Jonson was constantly brought into contact with composers and performers in producing the masques. He had an opportunity to know the musical world. He was a conscious artist and prepared his songs to please composers. He knew the devices, the tricks, the laws and the principles of song-writing.

There is no way to measure Jonson's reaction to music. No psychological tests can be applied to determine his musical ability. We know that he was a man of letters, that he had the temperament of a pedantic scholar. There is nothing in his poetry to lead anyone to believe that he was a gifted musician. When free to write verse to his taste, he revelled in classic meters. But when Jonson found it necessary to prepare a lyric for music, he did so with charm and easy grace. The nearer his lyrics approach song-form, the more flowing, the more singable, the more readable the poetry. The greater the stress under which he labored to satisfy the musicians, the more tuneful the lyric. Music taught Jonson to write light, melodious verse, and to arrange the pattern of a masque.

Chapter I is a discussion of Jonson's song-forms, emphasizing the technical devices which made his verse peculiarly suitable for singing. The *Forest, Epigrams,* and *Underwoods* contain illustrations of Jonson's attempts to please the composers. In these collections of miscellaneous poems there are light, graceful, melodious songs, (like *Drink to me Only with thine Eyes*), which have been set to music. These smooth-flowing, symmetrical patterns present a striking contrast to the heavy, scholarly verse written for the printed page. The song-like qualities which attracted the composers were the same qualities which make a lyric easy to read, melodious for the speaking voice. Quite naturally, the more musical the stanza, the more we enjoy reading it aloud. And we find that the stanzas which were made for song are the same poems editors and collectors seek out for their anthologies.

They are the stanzas critics praise most highly for their lyrical excellence.

Chapter II is a study of the songs in the plays. Of these the elaborate songs were written for the Children's Companies. These little "eyases" were professional musicians, and capable of performing the most difficult songs. Their lines differ considerably from the simple stanzas intended for the amateur performers of the adult companies. Naturally the more elaborate the song-form, the more technical skill required in the song-writer, and the more melodious, the more graceful the lyric. Words written for a gifted musician contained liquid tones, vowels suitable to delicate tone-shading—while words written for amateur musicians depend upon dramatic ability, gesture, facial expression and narrative power. Words which can be sustained through trills, delays, suspensions, or modulations of voice, are musically pleasant and adaptable to the speaking voice. And words which must be sung rapidly to explain dramatic situation or to interpret plot, or connect links in the action, appeal to the intellect; they do not bear great verbal melody; they are akin to the words intended for the printed page.

In Chapter III, a study of the music in the masques presents Jonson's fully developed power over song-forms. All of Jonson's knowledge of song-form and of the dramatic values of music contribute to the construction of a masque. He writes exquisite lyrics to be set to music. He places a treble next to a tenor solo to secure contrast of character or situation. Opening with stately prelude, or the giddy overture of satyrs, the first songs in the masques, like our own operas, prepare the audience for forth-coming events. The plot goes forward, or is delayed, by means of dialogue songs or soliloquies. Finally in the gradual swell of a full chorus, Jonson's great effects ensemble bring the masque to a conclusion. Treble, alto, tenor and bass rise with repeated refrains, mingling in many parts, in many rhythms, in exhilarating crecendos, smoothly drawn out cadences, to the triumphant climax. A full chorus concludes a masque with a definite sense of finality, a feeling of completeness, grandeur, repose.

CHAPTER I

SONG–FORMS

PART I. GENERAL PROBLEMS OF SONG-WRITING

There is a temptation to regard the poets of the Mermaid as divinely gifted wits, jovially tossing off madrigals as artlessly as they quaffed their bowls of sack and canary. Such spontaneity, and irresponsibility, were not, however, incompatible with an acquired mastery over the technicalities of music. It is not impossible that the most debonair songster was the most deeply steeped in the basic principles of harmony.

Many of the song-writers were themselves musicians. Drummond strummed sad sweet tunes on his lute; Lyly was choir-master of the singing boys of St. Paul's; Campion was both composer and performer. Others, like Samuel Daniel and John Milton, were brought up in musical households. They studied and absorbed music even as children. Ben Jonson laboriously mastered his art, at least so far as he needed it for his business. He searched everywhere for information concerning the music of the ancients; he became familiar with the Pythagorean theories, and traced out Plato's opinions on the doctrine of sound. He turned the pages of song-books, music primers, and manuscripts to gain knowledge from literary sources. He was the friend of composers and performers and gained what information he could from his contemporaries.

No matter how the poets acquired their knowledge of harmony, they observed and followed the dictates of musical law in their song-writing. Their very success is in itself evidence of a desire " to marry the words and the notes lovingly together." [1] They " designed their verses proper for music, the lyre and other instruments," [2] sometimes singing aloud as they penned their stanzas. An examination of the laws of Elizabethan music reveals what the composers demanded in the words they set to music, and shows us what the poets were trying to do to please the musicians.

[1] *The Works of Dr. Thomas Campion,* Ed. by A. H. Bullen, Chiswick Press, London, 1889, p. 45.

[2] See the quotations on page 9.

In the first place, the musicians wanted simple themes which touched their emotions and expressed their feelings. They wanted songs of universal appeal, not songs like Jonson's personal lines on the picture he had left in Scotland.[3] The most suitable words for singing should be easily understood when slurred, cut off quickly by a staccato chord, prolonged, delayed, or trilled. Stock phrases were preferable to subtle figures of speech, for the composers wanted to express the most delicate shades of emotional meaning in the notes. Words should suggest feeling, not explain ideas. Composers despaired of providing suitable accompaniment for argument, twisted thought, complex opinions, or philosophical data. The musicians chose stanzas made up of the by-words of sonneteers, religious divines, patriots, or nature lovers. For instance, a love song was frequently a eulogy of feminine beauty, a description of a demure or dashing mistress. " Golden tresses," " starry eyes " and " ruby lips " were again and again the theme of sonneteer and song writer. If a listener failed to hear " starry eyes " but understood " golden tresses " he could supply meanings for the words he had missed. His appreciation for some Delia, Celia, or Stella became identified with the melody; his thoughts soared beyond the realm of words into the realm of music, which is just what the composer desired.

Whatever the theme, the stanza was short. The fewer the words, the greater the composer's liberty in interpreting them. A short stanza allowed the composer to use many repetitions, variations and elaborations of the same theme. By this I do not mean that the musicians would have been happier without words. For the composers desired enough material to suggest emotion, mood or feeling,—enough to start the fancy roving; but not enough to burden the imagination nor enough to prevent variations and repetitions. A long poem required a long theme, and a long theme was apt to be monotonous.

Fa-la-la songs were popular because the words suggested a light playful feeling, and the composer could repeat his themes when he liked without injuring the sense; he could give undivided attention to melody and harmony, with no obligation to stress specific sentences. Songs should not be long enough to strain the voice, or wear out the singers. For polyphonic settings, composers preferred not more than eight or ten lines, as each phrase had to be

[3] *Underwoods.*

repeated three times.[4]   Harmonic songs, ayrs, or songs not requiring repetitions might be longer.

In addition to subject matter and length, the composer gave consideration to the type of musical setting which the words seemed to call for. He hoped to receive suggestions as to the general type of song-form which the poetry required. A long poem, suitable for a single voice was destined to solo arrangement with lute accompaniment. If the context implied dialogue, then two voices might sing alternately; if one speaker was a man, the other a woman, then the music required parts for a treble and a tenor, or a treble and a bass. If there were indications that two voices sang together, the composer harmonized the voices as a duet. Stanzas for more than two voices presented a choice between many kinds of harmonic and polyphonic settings.

There were many types of polyphonic song, among them the madrigal, the canzonet, the motet, and a number of other less familiar kinds—all of which had some points in common. The Elizabethans used their musical terms loosely, so that it is often difficult to differentiate between them.

The madrigal was the form of polyphonic music which was perhaps more than any other, the typical Tudor part-song. There is no brief and satisfactory way to define a madrigal. Dr. Fellowes has carefully discussed the various functions, the origin, and the development of madrigal singing.[5] Recent critics have taken into account the fact that the Elizabethans were not very careful to distinguish between the various forms of Tudor songs, and no one has seriously tried to limit the term *madrigal*. We usually think of a madrigal as a short poem, of approximately six lines, arranged to a musical setting for six, eight or ten voices, contrapuntally harmonized. The words suggested a definite mood, of a secular nature,—words which lent themselves to repetitions, changes of rhythm and other devices practised by Elizabethan composers.

A canzonet might be called a little madrigal, for the canzonet was much like a madrigal except that it was shorter and the musical setting simpler. The poem was usually five lines long,

[4] " It was a very general, but by no means strict practice for each voice to repeat a phrase three times."—Fellowes, Edmund H., *English Madrigal Composers*, Stainer and Bell, London, 1921, p. 52.

[5] Edmund Horace Fellowes, *The English Madrigal,* Oxford University Press, London, 1925.

the words were sung by three or possibly five voices. Changes of rhythm, repetitions and the other devices of madrigal composition which will be discussed later, were typical also of the canzonet.

A motet was also much like a madrigal, the chief difference being that a motet was religious rather than secular in theme, and that the music was more solemn and dignified in character.

Harmonic part-songs were usually short poems set to music composed of several parts; these parts each carried a melody which harmonized with the other parts of the song. Although there might be changes of rhythm, repetitions, etc., the harmonic part song was much simpler in structure. The voices were more apt to sing the same words at one time, so that there was no great dovetailing of voices. The elaborate devices of polyphonic music were not associated with harmonic songs; the chief difference between a sixteenth century harmonic part song, and our part song of today is that in Tudor times the melody was not of more importance than the other voices and the beauty of the song lay in the effect ensemble. Today, we emphasize a melody, and subordinate the other parts to the main theme.

It is refreshing to turn from a consideration of the abstract terminology of song-form, to Morley's appealing description of the way an Elizabethan song should sound: " you must in your music be wavering like the wind, sometime wanton, sometime drooping, sometime grave and staide, otherwile effeminate; . . . and shew the uttermost of your variete, and the more variete you shew, the better you shall please." [6]

Subject matter, length, and form have presented problems for the consideration of song-writers of all generations. Naturally we should expect to find that the poets of the sixteenth century were subject to these general problems of song writing. But in examining their stanzas we are particularly interested in the specific devices which they employed to please the Elizabethan composers. There were certain modes of expression, certain characteristics of song, certain fads, fashions and tendencies which were either peculiar to Elizabethan composers, or which reached their greatest development in the English music of the sixteenth

[6] Thomas Morley, *A Plaine and Easie Introduction to Practickall Musicke,* 1597, reprinted in 1608. This quotation is found on page 180 of the third part of the 1608 edition. (Drexel Collection, New York Public Library.)

century—these helped to distinguish Elizabethan song from the song of other ages.[7]   Passing from this brief description of the more general problems of song writing, let us next examine the peculiarly Elizabethan characteristics of song which affected the poetry of one of the most successful of Elizabethan song-writers.

Part II.   Technical Devices

If you could hear a group of hearty Elizabethans singing *Oh Hunter! from the forest green!*[8] you might think each man tried to out-sing his brother in lusty rivalry.   Polyphonic singing resembled an endurance contest in which several voices attempted to exceed each other in extravagance of repetition.   Every singer repeated the words over and over, warbling endlessly as if prevented from concluding the song.   Apparently the treble proceeded in this fashion:

Oh! Oh! Oh! hunter, hunter, hunter, Oh hunter! Oh hunter! Oh hunter!
Hunter from the forest, hunter from the forest, hunter from the forest,
Forest green, forest green, forest green; green, green, green . . .
    etc.

And while you strove to follow the treble's attempts through devious mazes of melody, you were aware that the tenor had begun in similar fashion, harmonizing his repetitions several pitches lower; long before you could gauge his progress, the cantus secundus had joined at another interval, and the bassus had picked up a fourth strain repeating the very same words.   The effect, though a bit confusing, was full of harmonic interest, and frequently of rare beauty.

[7] For an account of the reasons for the superiority of English music to the music of other countries in the sixteenth century, see Max Förster's article, " Shakespeare-Musik," *Der Germanisch Romanische Monatsschrift,* XVI, 1928, pp. 298–304.   This article also emphasizes the fact that Elizabethan music, though it contained elements of composition which were common to all ages, developed certain tendencies beyond those developed in other countries, etc.

[8] Dekker's song beginning *Oars, oars, oars, oars,* is one of the best examples of repetition in Elizabethan song. (*Westward Ho,* V. 1.)   Frequently poets constructed their lines in such a way that composers could separate the words into groups convenient for repetition; but Dekker quite obviously prepared his words for repetition.

By the time the song was ended, you were aware of the fact that repetition was one of the most popular devices of Elizabethan musical composition. Dr. Fellowes believed it a "very general, but by no means strict practice for each voice to repeat a phrase three times." [9] Certainly the composers were devoted to the practice, and poets observing their tendency humored their brother artists by preparing words suited to many kinds of repetition.

The use of an echo necessitated the repeating of words,—repeating in ways that pleased both poet and composer. From the poet's point of view, there was an advantage in using words which could be used again and again without changing the meaning, or seriously harming the meter. An echo was fitting material for pastoral poetry, and gave to the masque something of a bucolic touch; it awakened idyllic associations, stirred pastoral sentiments.[10]

There were also advantages for the composers. Echoes suggested contrasts in tonal shading, loud voices representing the original notes of the singer, with soft repetitions representing the echoes. The echo might be repeated in new pitches, in new keys, or with variations of the original. It was exceptionally convenient for the conclusion of a song, lending itself to a gradual diminuendo, each voice repeating a phrase more faintly until the melody came to rest on a last dim note of dying harmony. Jonson prepared for such a diminuendo by shortening the number of syllables in each succeeding line, so that the number of words was lessened in each line as the volume decreased. At the close of a song, the echo satisfied the listener, it brought the song to an ending of definite finality. The *Masque of Beauty* closes with a full song and echoing chorus:

[9] See the footnote on page 16 of this chapter.

[10] Thomas Heywood calls attention to the use of the echo in Act III of his *Silver Age:*

> Echoe, double all our lays,
> Make the champians sound, sound, sound,
> To the Queen of Harvest's praise,
> That sows and reaps our ground, ground, ground.

In the *Arraignment of Paris,* III, 5, Peele uses an echo song and comments upon the pleasing effect of the echo: "The grace of this song is in the shepherd's echo to her verse." Another example of an appropriately used echo in song, is in Act III. 1. of Davenant's *Unfortunate Lovers.*

Still turn and imitate the heaven
In motion swift and even;
 And as his planets go,
 Your brighter lights do so;
May youth and pleasure ever flow.
But let your State the while,
Be fixed as the isle.

Cho. So all that see your beauties sphere,
May know the Elysian fields are here.

1 *Ech.* The Elysian fields are here,
2 *Ech.* Elysian fields are here.

Echoes were not only appropriate conclusions to a song, but also they served as a means of dividing a stanza into symmetrical sections. Composers eagerly sought for ways of avoiding monotony and securing symmetry by separating their songs into sections. Sometimes they broke a polyphonic chorus by interspersing a few bars of homophonic music. Again a chorus might interrupt the onward movement of a duet or trio. Jonson very cleverly wove an echo into the body of a chorus, suggesting to the composer a very simple means of gaining symmetry and variety of expression. Jonson's description of the performance of such a song runs thus: " the musicians . . . came forth through the mazes to the other land: singing this full song, iterated in the closes by two Echoes, rising out of the fountains: "

When Love at first did move
From out of Chaos, brightened
So was the world, and lightened,
As now.
 1 *Ech.* As now!
 2 *Ech.* As now!
Yield Night, then to the light,
As BLACKNESS hath to BEAUTY:
Which is but the same duty.
It was for beauty that the world was made,
And where she reigns, Love's lights admit no shade.
 1 *Ech.* Love's lights admit no shade.
 2 *Ech.* Admit no shade.[11]

Jonson employed another device which closely resembled the echo, for the purpose of separating a song into sections. A short phrase might be placed within a stanza in such a way that it broke the monotony of a lengthy chorus. Like the echo, the short phrase

[11] *The Masque of Beauty, Masques and Entertainments, op. cit.,* p. 54.

could be repeated by several different voices, homophonically arranged.   Or if the composer chose, he might weave the phrase into the chorus by dove-tailing the words in polyphonic style.[12] In *Pan's Anniversary,* we find a song illustrating three uses for repetition: (1) an echo as a conclusion; (2) an echo, (homophonic music), for dividing a song into symmetrical sections; and (3) short phrases standing alone.[13]

Hymn III
                    If yet, if yet,
        Pan's orgies you will further fit,
    See where the silver-footed fays do sit,
            The nymphs of wood and water;
            Each tree's and fountain's daughter!
        Go take them forth, it will be good
        To see them wave it like a wood,
        And others wind it like a flood
                In springs,
                And rings,
        Till the applause it brings,
            Wakes Echo from her seat,
            The closes to repeat.

Ech.   The closes to repeat.
                    Echo the truest oracle on ground,
                        Though nothing but a sound.
Ech.   Though nothing but a sound.

[12] Fellowe's comments on this subject set forth the musical law more clearly: "The madrigalists were striving eagerly to devise some new kind of cohesion and symmetry of design in their compositions, and they adopted various methods for the purpose: thus, for instance, some of the more elaborate. . . are divided into two, or perhaps three, main sections by the introduction of a bar or two of homophonic, as contrasted with polyphonic, texture, the sub-sections being treated in the ordinary way, phrase by phrase, wthout any such interruptions of style.   This method of homophonic punctuation was a favorite device of Weelkes, and a good example is provided by that composer's *When Thoris Delights to Walk* (No. 2 of his Madrigals for Six voices); the poem is eight lines long and is divided by Weelkes into sections of two, four, and two lines, each section punctuated at its opening by a homophonic phrase." *Mad. Comp.,* p. 106.

[13] There is an interesting illustration of the use of short phrases in Beaumont and Fletcher's song, *Cynthia to thy power and thee, Maid's Tragedy,* I, 1.   Fletcher employed the same device again in *All ye woods, and trees, and bowers, Faithful Shepherdess,* V, 1 and in the song *Arm, arm, arm, Mad Lover,* V, 1.   Shirley employs this device in his song beginning *The Glories of our Blood and State, Cont. of Ajax and Ulysses.* See also Barten Holyday's *The Black Jack, Technogamia,* III, 5.

	Beloved of Pan the valleys' queen.
Ech.	The valleys' queen.
	And often heard, though never seen.
Ech.	Though never seen.[14]

Words or phrases standing alone, (for purposes of repetition), might also serve a dramatic purpose. In a song from *Pleasure Reconciled* Jonson wished to signal the masquers to come down from the top of a mountain, and he needed some emphatic means of signifying the moment of their descent. He separated the first two parts of the song by two short phrases, and the second and third parts by the word *descend*. The device was imitated by Shirley in his *Triumph of Peace,* though Shirley went a step further by indicating that solo voices could sing the emphatic words. Probably Shirley recognized the common practice of the musicians of thrusting a bar of homophonic music into a chorus and he was but enticing the composers to follow their own alluring practices. Jonson's *descends* gave the composer a chance to introduce a chorus; the various parts might take up the *descends,* voice by voice interweaving the repetitions of many parts into a well-joined link connecting the separated sections.

Jonson's Song [16]

Ope, aged Atlas, open then thy lap,
And from thy beamy bosom strike a light
That men may read in the mysterious map
ALL SIGNS
AND SIGNS,
Of royal education, and the right,
See how they come and show
That are but born to know.
DESCEND,
DESCEND;
Though pleasure lead,
Fear not to follow:
They who are bred
Within the hill
Of skill,
May safely tread
What path they will,
No ground of good is hollow.

[14] *Pan's Anniversary,* op. cit., p. 337.
[16] *Pleasure Reconciled to Virtue, op. cit.,* pp. 227, 228.

Shirley's Song [17]

(Duet sung by Irene and Eunonia)
We
Diche, have stayed expecting thee
Thou gavest perfection to our glory,
And seal to this night's story;
Astrea shake the cold dew from thy wing

Eu. (alone)   D E S C E N D
Ir.   "   D E S C E N D
Eu.   Descend and help us sing
The triumph of Jove's upper court abated
And all the deities translated.

There is another aspect of Elizabethan music which we have touched upon in connection with the principle of repetition illustrated by Shirley's and Jonson's *descend* songs. We have already discovered how the *descends* in Jonson's song separated the stanza into sections, and how the *descends* in Shirley's song contrasted with the duet sections preceding and following them. The composers were always seeking for ways and means to obtain symmetry and cohesion of design in their song patterns: some of the more elaborate songs (like Shirley's *descend*-song) were divided into two or three sections by the introduction of a bar or two of homophonic as contrasted with polyphonic texture.[18] Ordinarily the voices never came together at the end of a musical section unless the section also concluded the song.[19] One voice always carried on the melody, though the other voices might take brief rests, (joining later by repeating words of the homophonic measures, and dovetailing the phrases to another section). A better example of the use of alternating homophonic, and polyphonic singing than Shirley's and Jonson's already cited, occurs in *Mercury Vindicated*. The song is a dialogue between Prometheus and Nature, with strains of polyphonic music interspersed to avoid monotony.[20]

[17] *The Triumph of Peace,* James Shirley,—Dramatic Works with Notes by William Gifford, Pub. Alexander Dyce, London, 1833.

[18] *English Madrigal Composers, op. cit.,* pp. 106, 107. Also see footnote on page 21 of this chapter.

[19] *Ibid.*

[20] John Lyly's *Endymion* contains a song beginning "Stand who goes there," which is sung in dialogue with polyphonic measures interrupting the conversation. Lyly uses the same device in "O yes, O yes," *Galatea,* IV, 2, in Rixula's and the four pages' song, *Mother Bombie,* III, 4. See also, William Cartwright's use of dialogue with chorus in the *Royal Slave,* III, 1. See also, Ford's *Broken Heart,* "Glories, pleasures, pomps," V, 2, and Shakespeare's "You spotted snakes," *Mid. Sum. Night's Dream,* III.

Pro.   What! have you done   (Homophonic)
                          So soon?
                And can you from such beauty part?
                You'll do a wonder more than I.
                I woman with her ills did fly;
                But you their good, and them deny.

Cho.   Sure each hath left his heart   (Polyphonic)
          In pawn to come again, or else he durst not start.
Nat.   They are loth to go   (Homophonic)
                I know
        Or sure they are no sons of mine.
                There is no banquet, boys, like this,
                If you hope better, you will miss;
                Stay here, and take each one a kiss.
Cho.   Which if you can refine,   (Polyphonic)
        The taste knows no such cates, nor yet the palate wine
                No cause of tarrying shun,
        They are not worth his light, go backward from the sun.[21]

Perhaps the most appealing use of repetition is that in which
the first theme appears again as the last. In modern music,—
opera, sonata, symphony—we experience distinct pleasure at the
repetition of some familiar motif, especially if the motif occurs
in the overture of an opera, and again in the closing chorus.
Such symmetry and balance appeal to us in a song, and Jonson
uses the device by concluding with the same couplet he used at
the beginning. The opening couplet,

            O know to end, as to begin;
            A minute's loss in love is sin.

of the following song, quite possibly suggested the main theme
of the music, to the composer. The lines are undoubtedly the key
to the song, the essence of the thought, and the main theme of
the poem. These lines are repeated with but slight changes at the
end: (The italics are mine.)

            O know to end, as to begin:
            A minute's loss in love is sin.
            These humors will the night outwear
            In their own pastimes here;
            You do our rites much wrong,
            In seeking to prolong
            These outward pleasures:

[21] *Mercury Vindicated*, p. 193.

The night hath other treasures
Than these though long concealed,
Ere day to be revealed.
Then, know to end, as to begin;
A minute's loss in love is sin.[22]

Jonson prepared for yet another form of musical repetition far more subtle than the use of an echo or repeating motive. The last four lines in the chorus concluding *Chloridia* are just enough like each other to suggest repetition to a composer, and just different enough in meaning and in variation of the consonant sounds to appeal to the ear. Instead of repeating *Chloris the queen of Flowers,* four times, Jonson offers the composer a chance to repeat his musical phrases, if he chooses, to four different sets of words; emphasizing the close of each line by rhyme:

Chorus   Let all applaud the sight!
               Air first, that gave the bright
               Reflections, Day or Night!
               With these supports of Fame
               That keep alive her name,
               The beauties of the Spring
               Founts, Rivers, everything,
               From the height of all,
               To the water's fall,
               Resound and sing
   The honours of his Chloris to the King!
               Chloris the Queen of Flowers;
               The sweetness of all Showers;
               The Ornament of Bowers,
               The top of Paramours![23]

Another device distinctive of the Elizabethan composers was the use of alternating rhythms. Sixteenth century part songs are sometimes confusing in their variety of rhythmic patterns.

[22] *Hymen,* p. 72. This kind of repetition was frequently employed by Dekker, in *Oars, Oars Oars* (see foot-note to page 14), also in "Virtue's branches wither," *Old Fortunatus,* in "O sweet content," *Patient Grisill.* See Anthony Munday's use of this kind of repetition in the song in the third act of *John a Kent and John a Cumber;* also Middleton's "Weep eyes, break heart," *A Chaste Maid of Cheapside,* V, and in the *Widow,* IV, 2, the songs beginning "Give me fortune," III, 2, and "How around the world you go," III, 2.

[23] *Chloridia, op. cit.,* p. 374. Compare the ending of John Fletcher's song which begins "Arm, arm, arm . . .", from the *Mad Lover,* V, 1.

For instance, the treble might change from a three-four rhythm
to a two-four measure; or the treble might be singing a six-eight
bar while the other parts were singing in four-four time.   Sudden
alterations in rhythm occurred in unexpected places, and singers
had to" acquire facility for recognizing and conforming " to
them.[24]   While the composers " delighted " in such a " variety
of rhythms," a poet could do little to prepare for these changes.
Usually the composer twisted the words to conform to his musical
measures; but one device gave freedom to the composers without
risking great destruction to the poet's lines.   This was to con-
struct the lines of the song of uneven lengths, so that short
lines could be drawn out and delayed, and long lines could be set
to more rapid flights of notes.   The first song of Milton's *Comus*
beginning " Sweet Echo, sweetest Nymph, that liv'st unseen " [25]
illustrates the variety of line lengths used in songs where changes
of rhythm occurred in the musical setting.   Lawes changed the
stress in the lines, " By slow Meander's margent green," [26] probably to emphasize a dramatic feeling for a slow-moving tide.
Ferrabosco's setting to *Come my Celia*,[27] and *Still to be neat,
Still to be dressed*,[28] show changes of rhythm in every few measures.   Jonson's stanzas are particularly adapted to changes of
rhythm because of the irregularity of his line lengths.   The following song from the *Fortunate Isles* offers exceptional opportunities to changes of rhythm in the musical setting:

Pro. Ay, now the heights of Neptune's honours shine,
    And all the glories of his greater style
    Are read, reflected in this happiest isle.
Por. How both the air, the soil, the seat combine

[24] Fellowes illustrates what is meant by changing rhythm by an excerpt
taken from Moreley's *Though Philomela lost her love*, (Three part Canzonets, No. 23).   *Eng. Mad. Comp.*, p. 135.

[25] *Comus*, in *English Poems by John Milton*, Ed. R. C. Browne, Oxford
at the Clarendon Press, 1906, p. 54, Vol. I.
[26] Henry Lawe's Setting for *Comus*, Brit. Mus. MS. Add. 11518.
[27] Alphonso Ferrabosco's *Book of Ayres*, 1609.   (Brit. Mus.)
[28] See John Playford's *Select Ayres and Dialogues*, 1669.

To speak it blessed!
Sar.   These are the true groves
Where joys are born,
Pro.   Where longings,
Por.   And where loves!
Sar. That live!
          That last!
Por.   No intermitted wind
Blows here, but what leaves flowers or fruit behind.
Cho. 'Tis odour all that comes!
And every tree doth give his gums.

In the fourth song of the *News from the New World,* there are two short words concluding each cadence which suggest a break or change in the rhythms of the music.

Fourth Song
Look, look already where I am,
         Bright Fame,
Got up unto the sky,
         Thus high
Upon my better wing,
         To sing
The knowing king,
And made the music here,
With yours on earth the same.[29]

Closely akin to problems of alternating rhythms, was the problem of rhyme schemes. If a rhyme-ending fell at the end of a musical cadence, the composer had no cause for worry. But if the rhyme-ending fell within the cadence, or stretched beyond the end of the cadence the composer was compelled to fill in extra words, or to cut out offending syllables as the case might be. When a rhyme-ending fell exactly on a musical cadence ending, the result produced a sensation of completeness and satisfaction greatly to be desired. The first rhyming word of a couplet usually fell on a dominant or some chord leading to a concluding chord. The second rhyme-ending naturally fell on a tonic. Thus a couplet completed a thought on the second rhyme-ending just as the musical cadences found rest on the chord of finality. The

[29] Compare the broken rhythmic effects, the short line lengths, the irregularities of line in Dekkar's *Haymakers, rakers,* etc. (Sun's Darling, III); with Fletcher's *Away, delights* (The Captain, III, 4); Shirley's *Woodmen, shepherds, come away* (The School of Compliment, V); and Marston's *O Love, how strangely sweet* (The Dutch Courtesan, V, 1).

following lines show how one chord might lead to another in completing the stanza, while a slight delay emphasizes the concluding chord:

> Beauties have ye seen a toy? (dominant)
> Called Love, a winged boy? [30] (tonic)

At the word *toy* the musical phrase is suspended a moment on a dominant chord, with an unfinished, expectant effect. The final cadence concludes, (comes to rest) on a tonic on the word *boy*. The chief thing to remember in connection with rhyme-schemes and musical cadences, is that the rhyming words are emphasized either by having them fall on the same tone, making a repetition of tones,[31] or by having the first rhyming word fall on a dominant or some tone leading into tonic. The resolution, naturally falls on the last word of the rhyme.

Undoubtedly the composer studied the rhythms of the lines and the rhyme schemes, but he felt at liberty to change both at will. There was not much that the poet could do to prepare for alternating rhythms and the resolution of chords. He indicated the mood, the atmosphere to be suggested by musical settings in the words, sometimes in the verbal melody. *O's* and *Ah's* and *OO's* are potentially melancholy, or regretful, or buoyant depending on the singer's interpretation. By means of careful tone-shading a singer can convert " Ah " into a long unhindered sigh, or an " O " into a desperate sob. On the other hand, quick staccato consonant sounds suggest rapid movement, mirth, lightness, playfulness. Jonson prepared *Slow, slow fresh fount* [32] as an expression of grief, and the songs of Oberon's fairies to stimulate mirth and sprightly gayety. Vowel sounds predominate in the former, quick, light consonant sounds, in the latter.[33]

---

[30] The words of this song were taken from *The Hue and Cry after Cupid,* p. 90, and the music is found in the British Museum, MS. Add. 11608.

[31] A good example of this is found in the Ferrabosco setting for " Yes were the loves or false or straying," Book of Ayres, 1609, when the words *straying* and *waying* fall on E . . . , the first an octave higher than the next.

[32] *Cynthia's Revels,* I, 1. This song compares in mood and in intensity of feeling, in dominancy of "O" sounds and liquids, with " Pardon Goddess of the night," *Much Ado,* V, and " Willow willow," Othello, IV, 3, with "Oh sorrow, sorrow," Samuel Rowley's *Noble Soldier,* I, 1 and Fletcher's " Weep no more, nor sigh, nor groan," Queen of Corinth, III, 2.

[33] *Masque of Oberon,* such songs as " Seek you Majesty to strike," p. 153, and " Nor yet, nor yet, you in this night blest," p. 154. These have

Although composers were ever searching for words suggestive
of feeling and emotion, they seem not to have sought for explicit
statements concerning mood or atmosphere. They interpreted
emotion according to their own feeling about the implied meaning. Jonson never gave vent to outbursts of emotion in his
poetry; he was one of the most restrained of the song writers.
He suggested the mood of his stanzas in his choice of words,
and through his verbal melodies, leaving the composer to elaborate
upon the suggestions, to emphasize the meaning in the music.
Slow slow fresh fount offered the composer exceptional opportunities to express sorrow. Jonson saw to it that the context as
well as the verbal melody suggested grief. Yet the poet in no
way hindered the composer by inserting unrestrained expostula-
tions, such as, " Hear my wailing cries." " Hear my wailing
cries " in Elizabethan times, would have demanded a descending
minor scale of tones, suggestive of actual sobbing. The composer
was free to emphasize the meaning, interpret the mood of the
mourner according to his own fancy.

The ballad of John Urson, a rollicking good-humored song for
dancing, is another example of Jonson's restrained power of suggestion. A composer could emphasize the lightness, and mirth
of the song, and add a buoyancy to the dance rhythm by stressing
the extra syllables in the third and sixth lines. John enters with
his bears who dance while he sings:

> Though it may seem rude
> For me to intrude,
> With these my bears my chance-a;
> 'Twere sport for a king,
> If they could sing,
> As well as they can dance-a.[34]

qualities in common with Lyly's " Pinch him, pinch him," *Endymion*, IV,
3. Palatal vowel sounds and dentals are also apparent in the examples just
noted.

[34] *Masque of Augurs:* p. 296. The " a " ending lent a suave dance rhythm
to songs which might otherwise not claim the mood and movement of
dancing. Many poets made use of the device with varying degrees of
success. See particularly Anthony Munday's version of a *Song of Robin
Hood*, in the *Triumph of Ancient Drapery*. See also the song beginning
" Round about " from the *Maid's Metamorphosis*, II, and the song in *Technogamia* Act III. Sc. 5. Shakespeare used the " a " ending effectively
in Jog on, Jog on, *Winter's Tale*, IV, 3; Will you buy any tape, *ibid*. IV, 4.

There is a suggestion of lightness and of fairy-like charm in the delicate songs of the masque of Oberon. Alliteration, short staccato consonant sounds, and short syllables strike a word melody adaptable to graceful stringed accompaniment. Beginning with two dainty, pricking syllables, words trip along through delicate imagery, each line increasing in the number of its syllables to a spritely climax.

> Nay, nay,
> You must not stay,
> Nor be weary yet;
> This is no time to cast away,
> Or for fairies so to forget
> The virtue of their feet.
> Knotty legs and plants of clay
> Seek for ease, or love delay,
> But with you it still should fare
> As with the air of which you are.[35]

"Another essential feature of the English madrigalists, like that of their Italian predecessors in the same century, was the introduction, at the end of each section, of a florid rhythmical passage vocalized to the syllables Fa-la-la. Occasionally some other syllable was substituted. Weelkes used *No, no, no,* in *Say Dainty Nymphs, Shall we go Play?* (No. 9 of his Ballets) and Morley gave *lirum lirum* for the refrain of *You that wont my pipes to sound* (Morley's Ballets No. 13)."[36] Composers seized upon any word for such a passage that could emphasize the feeling of emotional interest in the composition. Dekker chose a *thwick-thwack* chorus for his *Hammer Song.*[37] Shakespeare used *heynonino* in *It was a lover and his lass,*[38] and *willow, willow, willow* for Desdemona's plaint.[39] Campion's *No, no, no, no, no*[40] as well as Jonson's *no, no, no* in *If she forsake me,*[41] served the

---

[35] *Oberon*, p. 154. Compare in the structure of line lengths and lightness of touch with *I obey, I obey,* in Fletcher's *Humorous Lieutenant,* IV. 3; and *Come let the state stay,* Sir John Suckling's *Discontented Colonel,* II.

[36] Fellowes, *Eng. Mad. Comp., op. cit.,* p. 57.

[37] *London Tempe.*

[38] *As You Like It,* V, 3.

[39] *Othello,* IV, 3.

[40] *First Book of Ayres,* from the *Works of Thomas Campion, op. cit.* p. 37.

[41] Jonson's *No, no, no* refrain occurs in a song from *Love Freed, op. cit.,* p. 165.

same purpose.   Jonson also contributed a *still, still, still* chorus at
the close of each of the six songs composing the main body of his
Masque for the Honour of Wales.[42]

Here and there through the old song-books there were very
obvious traces of a peculiarity of the composers, which for good
reasons Dr. Fellowes has called "pictorial treatment." A cradle
song might appear in notation as a wavering series of notes resembling a billowy rocking.   Similarly, the flight of birds might
be pictured by notes of rising and falling tune,[43] or a song about
Aetna's flames inspire a line of notes resembling pointed spires
of fire.[44]   The word *sigh* was very generally preceded by a rest
in order to enhance its realistic effect, but whereas such treatment
occasionally led very near to paths of triviality there can be no
such feeling associated with the word used by Gibbons at the
word *death* in the *Silver Swan* (No. 1. of his Madrigals) or
still more remarkable chord which Weelkes wrote at the word
dead in his *Noel Elegy* (No. 10 of his six-part Madrigals).   This
was the type of detail the madrigal composers studied and cared
for, rather than any conventional subserviency to musical rule
or to formality of design, and it was this feature which enabled
them to achieve such glorious success." [45]

Elizabethan song is full of words suited to many kinds of
pictorial treatment.   Henry Lawes set Milton's *Comus* to tunes
which were very rich in this kind of dramatic value.[46]   The line
From the heavens now I fly [47] contains the leap of melody of one
octave from a low tone to a high one on the one word *fly*.   The
line *Up in the broad fields of the sky* [48] agrees with a series of
quarter notes contrasting with previous eighths to emphasize
breadth and fullness, while the entire musical phrase is composed
of high notes suggesting the rare atmosphere of high altitudes.

[42] *For the Hon. of Wales, op. cit.,* p. 237–38.

[43] *Fellowes, op. cit.,* p. 108.

[44] *Ibid.* References to fire and burning were very frequent. Shakespeare's "Fie on sinful fantasy," *Merry Wives,* V, 5, contains a good example of the use of the word: "Whose flames aspire, higher and higher."
Caliban sings, "fetch a firing," *Temp.* III, 2. Peele uses *fire* three times
in the song of the Prologue to the *Love of King David.* Jonson uses the
word again and again in songs which I shall later discuss.

[45] *Ibid.*

[46] See footnote 26, page 26 of this chapter.

[47] *Ibid.*

[48] *Ibid.*

The last phrase of the last song in *Comus*, " Would stoop to her,"
is represented by a drop in the melody from high notes to low notes
in imitation of the action of stooping. Milton's songs show far
too many indications of pictorial treatment to require further
comment. It is equally easy to discover the same tendencies
throughout Jonson's songs. As I touch upon various songs here
and there through this study, I will point out the words peculiarly
adapted to pictorial notation. The song, *Daughters of the subtle
flood*,[49] contains the words *longer, longer, longer* each one repeated
in a succeeding line, and each one offering many opportunities
for a fully drawn out cadence, a decided delay in the tempo or
a series of whole or half notes. *Flood* might be accompanied
by rising and swelling melody imitating an oncoming tidal wave.
Quickly, flight, follow, flee, are potential in suggestivity of trills,
runs and grace notes.[50]

Repetitions, alternating rhythms, suggestions of mood, fal-la-la
passages, and words suggestive of pictorial treatment,—these were
the devices which Elizabethan poets provided to satisfy the requirements of the composers. Now let us observe how Jonson
employed these devices to secure lyric quality in his poetry.

[49] *Masque of Blackness, op. cit.,* p. 43.

[50] Words suggesting changes of tempo were very frequent in Elizabethan
song. " Lingeringly " is gently drawn out to express the feeling of slow
movement, Beaumont and Fletcher's song: " 'Tis mirth that fills the veins,"
Knight of the Burning Pestle, II, 1. See Dekkar's use of " lengthens " in
" Cast care away," *The Sun's Darling. Arise* on the other hand was often
set to a rising of the tune with quickening of the tempo, as Schubert
used arise in " Hark! hark! the Lark." Dekkar repeats *arise* in the Schubert fashion in *Beauty arise, The Patient Grissill.* Perhaps the word
which had the most picturesque musical connotation in Elizabethan song,
was the word *wanton.* The word was usually set to a series of grace
notes following a wavering tune. This excerpt is taken from Ferrabosco's notes for " If all   W - A - N - T - O - N
the cupids now were blind,"
Masque of Beauty. " Love
is blind and a *wanton* " is an-
other Jonsonian illustration
of the use of this word.
(*Poetaster*, IV. 3.) Other examples can be found in Nabbes " Of *Wanton
Art* " *Hannibal and Scipio,* III. 5; Heywood's " Refrain ye pretty *wantons,*" *Fair Maid;* Dekkar's " Sleep pretty *wantons* " Patient Grissill; Middleton's " Did Jove but see this *wanton* eye," *Blurt Master* V. Lodge's
" *Wanton* thou" *Looking glass for London,* and Lyly's " Oh Cupid,"
Mother Bombie.

PART III. SONGS IN THE MISCELLANEOUS COLLECTIONS

The lyrics in Jonson's collections, *Epigrams, Underwoods,* and the *Forest* might be classified under four headings: the lyrics which were set to music, the lyrics which have song form but were not set to music, the poems which were never intended to be sung, but which have certain qualities in common with songs, and the poems which have neither song form nor qualities in common with songs.

The poems in the first group have been chosen from time to time by editors and critics of lyric verse, and printed in collections of Elizabethan poetry. We may examine these poems in order to discover how Jonson used his knowledge of musical technicalities in the writing of songs.

The poems of the second group might easily attract a composer. There is no record that they were ever set to music; but they sing themselves, they are rich in verbal melody, and they bear the marks of Elizabethan song-form. They, too, are sought out by editors and collectors of Elizabethan verse because of their lyrical beauty.

The poems of the third group were never intended to be sung, but they bear resemblances to songs. They differ from the poems of the preceding groups in being less popular with anthologists, in having less pleasing verbal melody, and in having fewer of the qualities and characteristics commonly attributed to songs.

The poems of the last group scarcely deserve to be called lyrics, though some of them approach pleasing verbal melody at times, and perhaps Jonson regarded them as lyrics. An author is not always the best judge of his own work. These poems are full of erudite allusions, biographical data, and historical fact. Anthologists do not include these verses in their collections. The lines do not resemble song, either in subject matter or in form. Jonson did not intend them to be sung, and musical settings could not be adapted to them.

Group I. The Songs which Were Set to Music

Naturally the first song to consider in connection with Ben Jonson is the well known lyric, *Drink to me only with thine eyes.*[51] Few songs in the English language have been so widely praised

[51] *The Forest.*

for lyric beauty and exquisite harmony of notes and music. Both poets and musicians have lauded the delicacy of the verbal melody, the artless appeal of the notes, and the graceful combination of the verse and music.

The words, based upon certain lines of Philostratus' Epistles,[52] are arranged in a pattern of great lyric beauty. No one has been able to analyze the qualities which enabled Jonson to weave out of the straggling passages of the Epistles, the delicate lines of *Drink to me only.* Musicians have been equally at a loss to account for the mysterious composition of the notes. For many years, the name of the composer was unknown, but critics now attribute the piece to Colonel Mellish.[53] There is an anonymous setting for the song in manuscript form, in the British Museum,[54] which throws but little light on the question. From time to time, the notes have been accredited to Mozart, for critics believed that no other composer was capable of arranging so delightful, and so suitable a setting.

There are reasons, however, for thinking that possibly the tune as we know it, was in existence before Jonson adapted his words to it. Though it was generally Jonson's custom to write words which were later set to music, in one or two instances, he selected tunes which were already popular, and wrote words to fit the notes. Such was the case, perhaps, in the ballad beginning " My master and friends and good people draw near," from *Bartholomew Fair,* which Chappell thinks was set to the old tune of *Paddington's Pound.*[55] " You woeful wights give ear a while " from the *Case is Altered,* was probably similarly arranged to the popular old tune, *The Children in the Wood.*[56] Moreover, in *Cynthia's Revels,* Act IV, Scene 1, Jonson shows that he was familiar with the problems of fitting syllables to notes, when Amorphus comments on the difficulties of marrying ascending syllables to ascending notes, and descending syllables to descending notes.

In contending that Jonson used an old tune, I do not wish to

[52] Philostrautus' Epistles, XXIV, XXX, XXXI.

[53] For a bibliography of the research done on this subject, consult *The Song Index* ed. Minnie E. Searles, W. H. Wilson and Co. New York, 1926, p. 14.

[54] Anonymous setting, Brit. Mus. ms. Add. 29386, fol. 12b (Eighteenth century?).

[55] See Chapter II, p. 69, footnote 41.

[56] William Chappell, *Popular Music of the Olden Time,* Vol. I, p. 201.

imply that Colonel Mellish had no part in the development of the setting as we know it. The melody is of some vital song stuff which outlasts fashions of notation. It may have been hummed years before Jonson was born, years before Mellish gave it its final form; certainly it has been arranged and re-arranged many times since.

Another reason for thinking that Jonson wrote the words for *Drink to me only with thine eyes* to a tune that was popular in his day, is that he usually prepared songs to suit an elaborate song pattern, while he wrote the words to this song for a very simple pattern. Most of Jonson's songs bear evidences that he prepared them with an eye to what the composers might do to his stanzas. He anticipated changes of rhythm, repetitions, pictorial treatment etc., in fact, he wrote with a view to polyphonic settings, or àt least settings which required the accompaniment of lute or viol. But *Drink to me only with thine eyes* is utterly simple; there are no traces that Jonson expected a composer to set these lines to music. There are no preparations for repetitions, changes of rhythm, pictorial treatment, etc.

My conclusion is that Jonson picked out a tune that pleased him, and by sheer craftsmanship fitted the words to the notes achieving a union of music and poetry that is hard to parallel in the history of English song. Having once caught the verbal melody of *Drink to me only with thine eyes,* Jonson tried again and again to ensnare it in his other songs, songs which we will discuss later in this chapter,—so that with slight verbal variations, we can sing a number of Jonson's lyrics to the tune of *Drink to me only with thine eyes.*

In contrast to the simplicity of *Drink to me only,* the little song, *Follow a Shadow,* bears many traces of elaborate polyphonic setting. This is the type of song which Jonson prepared to please the composers of his day. He anticipated changes of rhythm, repetitions, and words suited to pictorial treatment. The first line is suited to many repetitions. The treble might sing: Follow, follow, follow a shadow, etc. (see page 43). " Follow, follow, follow a shadow, follow a shadow, follow a shadow, it still still still still flies you, still flies you," etc. Each line suggests similar repetitions. The pauses fall gracefully near the middle of each line. The last lines are divided into thirds, for variety, and to show differences between the concluding lines and those directly preceding. The lines are of irregular lengths, allowing the composer liberties in altering rhythms. There are abundant opportunities also, for pictorial treatment,—*flies* occurs twice. (Recall what Henry Lawes did to the word, page 31 of this chapter.) *Follow,* also holds out possibilities for gentle flights of grace notes, while *alone* calls for a majestic chord. *Longest* might give rise to a well delayed measure, with *strongest* corresponding to a swelling volume of sound.

As far as I know, there is no record for any musical setting for this song earlier than Sir Hubert Parry's,[57] but there is no reason to believe the song was not set to music and sung during Jonson's life. Parry, who was an enthusiastic admirer of Elizabethan music was probably attracted to the song because of its suggestion of delicacy, fragility, and the dainty verbal melody which is delightfully in keeping with the subject matter. In his setting, Parry tried to carry out the Elizabethan ideals of notation, emphasizing repetitions, changes of rhythm and variations, etc., in interpreting the words.

Although *Come my Celia,* from *Volpone,* and *Have you seen but a white lily grow?* from *The Devil is an Ass,* occur in the miscellaneous collections of Jonson's poetry, and might be included in the present discussion, these songs were originally prepared for plays, and will therefore be considered in Chapter II.

I sing the birth,[58] is so far as we know, the only one of Jonson's religious songs which received musical setting. It is symmetrically arranged in four stanzas for harmonic part singing. The lines fall smoothly in cadences suited to singing, and are pleasing when read aloud. Jonson was noted more as a tavern roisterer than a religious mystic, yet this song is a sincere expression of devotion, and may well have inspired Randolph's tribute:

> But if heaven take thee, envying us thy lyre,
> 'Tis to pen anthems for an Angel's Quire.[59]

Compared with the short choppy lines of *Hear me O God,*[60] and the harsh rasping verbal melody of *O Blessed Glorious Trin-*

---

[57] Parry, C. Hubert, *Follow a Shadow, English Lyrics,* Seventh Set, London, Novello and Co., 1907.

[58] *Underwoods.*

[59] Randolph, Thomas, *The Poems and Amyntas,* ed. J. J. Parry, Yale Univ. Press, New Haven, 1917, p. 84.

[60] *Underwoods.*

ity,[61] the words of *I sing the brith* have exquisite smoothness and are of singing quality.

Group II. Songs that Were Not Set to Music

Unfortunately composers are capricious in their choices of the words for their songs. Today, they are quite notorious for setting absurd lines to beautiful notes. In the Elizabethan period, composers may have been better critics of poetry, for they selected much of the best verse of the period for musical setting. Or they may have been merely fortunate in having so much good verse to choose from that they could not go far astray. Though they were often fortunate, they were by no means infallible; frequently they set poor stanzas to music, and certainly they overlooked a great deal of excellent song material. Jonson however fared well in this respect, for most of his songs were actually sung during his life. But for a number of his stanzas which would make very good songs no music has come down to us.

Oh do not wanton with those eyes [62] is unquestionably a charming lyric. Gifford judged it the best in the language. Other critics have praised it for its light rhythmic melody, and graceful imagery. Liquid consonants interwoven with resonant vowels and sibilants offer a singer opportunities for delicate tone-shading, for passionate vibrating modulations, for leisurely crescendos, and gentle diminuendos. The stanzas are identical metrically. This is one of the songs which, with slight syllabic alterations, could be sung to the tune of *Drink to me only.* The words are rich in pictorial suggestions. *Wanton* called for a wavering phrase of melody, with rising and falling notation. *Down* usually brought about a sudden drop in the scale, and *rise* was frequently set to an upward flight of notes.

Another song resembling the melodic pattern of *Drink to me only* is the stanza beginning *For Love's Sake, kiss me once again.*[63] The kinship is perhaps less apparent than that between *Drink to me only,* and *Oh do not wanton;* but the best test is to try singing all of these stanzas to the same tune. *For Love's sake* is also well adapted to singing purposes, the frequency of liquids, full and mellow vowel sounds, and questions and answers give a soloist al-

[61] *Underwoods.*
[62] *Ibid.*
[63] *Ibid.*

luring opportunities for vocalizing. An artist would find the song excellently prepared for tone-shading and delicate phrasing. The song is equally adaptable to madrigal setting, solo, or even harmonic arrangement. If the composer chose to arrange the song as a madrigal, the first line is well divided for repetitions: *For love's sake, for love's sake, for love's sake: Kiss me, kiss me, kiss me, once again, once again, once again . . .* etc. There are possibilities for light humour and charming playfulness, as well as lingering, long drawn out cadences. These stanzas, too, call for pictorial treatment. The word *kiss,* inasmuch as it is the key-word of the song, would probably be emphasized by notes suggesting the tone, or mood, of the entire composition. If the song is slow, insinuating, drawn out,[64] the word *kiss* might even be set to a minor chord, or if the piece is light, airy, frivolous, the same word might be arranged to a burst of dainty trills.[65] *Long* requires a delayed cadence, *in vain* a minor touch, *doubt* a series of wavering notes, *stay* a pause, or drawn out chord, *flies* a flight of grace notes, *lightly* to picking staccato tones, and *spy* a rising cadence of enquiry.

Kiss me sweet the wary lover [66] is similar in tone and expression to *Come my Celia let us prove.*[67]   With a few alterations it may be sung to the same tune. Naturally, *Kiss me sweet* has song-form. It also has been judged a good lyric by editors and anthologists, and might very well be set to music.

It is not growing like a tree,[68] *I love, and he loves me again,*[69] *Men if you love us play no more,*[70] and *Hang up those dull and envious fools* [71] could be very easily set to music. Their stanzas are of uneven line-lengths providing for changes of rhythm. The

[64] In the seventh song in Ferrabosco's *Book of Ayres,* " So leave off this last lamenting kiss," the word *kiss* is set to a minor " A," followed by a long drawn out minor chord on the lute. The " A " corresponding to *Kiss* in the melody, is a half note.

[65] In the anonymous setting of " Drink to me only with thine eyes," Brit. Mus. ms. Add. 29386 the word *kiss* is set to a dainty flourish of an eighth, a grace note and quarter.

[66] *The Forest.*

[67] Volpone, III, 2.

[68] An Ode to Sir Lucius Garry, and Sir H. Morison, Strophe III, *Underwoods.*

[69] *Underwoods.*

[70] *Ibid.*

[71] *Ibid.*

lines are broken into short phrases for musical cadences, or for
repetitions. They are suited to polyphonic settings, though *Men
if you love us* is equally well adapted to harmonic treatment.
The words are potentially pictorial. They have been popular
with collectors of lyric verse, and when read aloud they are rich
in verbal melody and musical suggestiveness.

Group III. *Stanzas which Are Related to Music but Were Never Intended for Singing*

Though Jonson's best lyrics echo the measures of Elizabethan
music, some of his poems are haunted by the strains of earlier
bards. In his odes, for instance, there are traces of a music
long dead; for Jonson closely adhered to classic models, like the
Pindaric odes. The great classic writers were themselves imitators
of earlier singers, singers who stroked the lyre as they chanted
their measures. Jonson's odes lack the vital magic of living
music, of Elizabethan song, but they echo faintly the rhythms of
far away cadences which have lost their tunes. Occasionally
there are surviving phrases of melody, but the stanzas as a whole
suggest contemplation rather than song. Such are a step removed
from first-hand intimacy with song, and a degree lower in a scale
of lyric appeal.

The stanza beginning *High spirited friend* [72] has verbal melody
in its opening lines. Beginning with the fifth and sixth lines, the
tune changes key and quavers rather weakly to the end. The
latter part of the poem is mainly the meditation of a philosopher,
calling for consideration, and concentration. Perhaps Jonson
tossed a few bars of verbal melody into the opening cadences but
became more interested in designing the pattern of an ode as he
proceeded, and forgot about Elizabethan song. The music is far
more like dead music, music dead since Pindar left stroking his
lyre.

Come let us here enjoy the shade, [73] and *Come with our voices
let us war,* [74] are less imitative and to a certain extent follow song-
form. They are symmetrically drawn up with parts apportioned
to various singers. They are not songs for singing,—but songs
representing poetic interpretations of singing. Nor are the stan-

[72] *Underwoods.*
[73] *Ibid.*
[74] *Ibid.*

zas to Edward Filmer [75] songs, though Jonson may have wished
to flatter the Queen's musician by imitating in words his song
cadences. The attempt, however, has never stirred the world,
either as a lyric or as a song.

The epitaph on the child actor, Salathiel Pavy,[76] is a sincere
expression of grief, interesting for its verbal melody. Critics
are drawn to this lyric because of its plaintive beauty, its sin-
cerity, its echoing of dead music. But after all, it is for meditation, not for singing; it causes us to think, not to weep. It is
without the vitality of song.

In addition to these attempts to make words suggest music,
there are poems which are touched here and there by the strains
of Elizabethan melody, but which ought not to be called songs.
They have song-form, but are lacking in true song-quality. In
writing these verses for music, Jonson was at fault in his selection
of material, at fault in trying to express, as songs, feelings and
ideas which were far removed from any kinship with the spirit
of song. For the most part, they are expressions of peculiarly
Jonsonian aspects of feeling, so that they appeal to our interest,
our intellect, or at times to our sense of humour, but not to our
emotions.

The lines about Jonson's picture left in Scotland are arranged
in song-form:

> I now think, Love is rather deaf than blind,
>   For else it could not be,
>   That she,
> Whom I adore so much, should so slight me,
> And cast my suit behind:
> I'm sure my language to her was as sweet,
> And every close did meet,
> In sentence of as subtle feet,
>   As hath the youngest he,
>   That sits in shadow of Apollo's tree
>   Oh! but my conscience fears,
>   That fly my thoughts between,
>   Tell me that she hath seen
>   My hundreds of gray hairs,
>   Told seven and forty years,
> Read so much waste, as she cannot embrace
> My mountain belly, and my rocky face,
> And all these through her eyes, have stopped her ears.[77]

[75] *Underwoods.*
[76] Epigram CXX.
[77] *Underwoods.*

The stanza is made up of lines of irregular length, suited to changes of rhythm, of short cadences suitable for repetitions, delicate musical phrasing, and interesting, if not altogether pleasing word music. *Sweet, slight, close,* and *fly* suggest pictorial settings.

The opening sentences lead us to think the song is a love-song, but before we have read far we discover that Jonson is poking fun at an incongruous love suit. For certainly the middle-aged poet had no serious intention of stirring a passion in the Scotch maiden's heart by alluding to his "mountain belly" and "rocky face." Though there is a touch of wistfulness in the poet's jesting it is hardly credible that he expected the song to be sung. The poem does not draw forth high praise from the critics, who leave it out of the anthologies.

Wretched and foolish jealousy,[78] like the lines on the picture left in Scotland, is clothed in song-form. There are provisions for alternating rhythms in the unequal line lengths, and preparations for repetitions in the short phrases, and the divided lines. There are two metrically identical stanzas. But the spring of emotion is dry. The lines may have been written from a sense of duty, or in a moment of contrition. But Jonson's passion against jealousy was little more than a passing sensation, and the feeling must have disappeared before the poem was finished. Recalling Jonson's war with Dekkar and Marston, his long feud with Inigo Jones, the poem resolves itself into a debate: Jonson's intellect expressing what his emotions denied. Unfortunately, not even Jonson's skill could clothe his poem with a semblance of genuine feeling. The presence of Inigo Jones at court was something of an obstacle to a flowing current of song against jealousy.

The stanza beginning *Or scorn or pity on me take* [79] is similar to the lines on jealousy in expressing a fictitious feeling. Apparently the lines are an embodiment of a dream of love. Now Jonson was not a dreamer any more than he was temperamentally averse to jealousy. When he dreamed, he may have seen armies marching to battle on his great toe, as he reported to Drummond; though he may have had visions of impossible wars and adventure, he was by nature disinclined to dream of love. His love-dream is insipid, and the expression of it without lyric appeal. No mat-

[78] *Underwoods.*
[79] *Ibid.*

ter how many song-devices Jonson could bring to bear to express his dream, he could not make a song out of a subject so foreign to his actual feeling.

On the whole, the poems of this group show various aspects of Jonson's ability as a song writer; but none of them reflects him at his best. To write a good song for singing Jonson required every bit of his song-craft, all of his technical skill, all of his power of judgment and selection.

Group IV. Songs without Music

When Jonson was at liberty to write as he pleased, he summoned his classic models, he arranged his great store-houses of myth, lore, and legend, and with a glass of canary wine, went somberly, if not soberly to his pleasures. Most of the poems in the miscellaneous collections are long, dull and wearisome. Composers would fall asleep setting them to music, and singers would strain their throats trying to sing them. The lines to *Penshurst* [80] and such stanzas as the *Epistle to Lady Katherine Aubigny* [81] are unquestionably solid, heavy, and monotonous. None of the long poems are akin to song in form or quality; and none of them have appeared in the anthologies.

The short poems which have not already fallen under discussion in Groups I, II and III appeal to the intellect. They are bookish rhymes about alchemy [82] usurers,[83] court scandal,[84] and teachers.[85] They are subtle in thought and pointed or twisted in meaning. They are made up of solid lines of even length, expressing little or no verbal melody. The words do not suggest tunes, nor pictorial treatment. After trying to sing these poems, if you are not sure about their song-quality, compare them as they appear on the printed page with the poems of Groups I and II. These intellectual stanzas look solid and heavy and regular in pattern. The Poems of Group I and Group II have more irregular borders, wavering patterns and designs, their very appearance is " sometimes drooping, sometimes staide," [85a] " sometimes a long

[80] *The Forest.*
[81] *Ibid.*
[82] Epigram VI.
[83] Epigram XXXI.
[84] Epigram XV.
[85] Epigram XIV to William Camden.
[85a] Morley, see footnote 6, p. 17.

line, sometimes a short one at choice of your ear." [86]   As types
of the two extremes compare the two following stanzas, and
you will observe that even a coldly printed page reflects something of the difference between a song, and a bit of Jonson's
contemplative erudite verse.

To Esme Lord Aubigny [87]—CXXVII

> Is there a hope that man would thankful be,
> If I should fail in gratitude to thee,
> To whom I am so bound, loved Aubigny?
> No, I do therefor call posterity
> Into the debt; and reckon on her head,
> How full of want, how swallowed up, how dead
> I and this muse had been, if thou hadst not
> Lent timely succours, and new life begot:
> So all reward or name that grows to me
> By her attempt, shall still be owing thee
> And than this same I know no abler way
> To thank thy benefits: which is to pay.

VIII.   Song That Women are but Men's Shadows [88]

> Follow a shadow it still flies you,
>   Seem to fly it, it will pursue:
> So court a mistress, she denies you.
>   Let her alone, she will court you.
> Say are not women truly, then,
> Styl'd but the shadows of us men?
> At morn and even shades are longest:
>   At noon they arc or short, or none:
> So men are weakest, they are strongest,
>   But grant us perfect, they're not known.
> Say are not women truly, then,
> Styl'd but the shadows of us men?

[86] Ronsard, see footnote 63 to p. 9, Introduction.
[87] *Epigrams.*
[88] *The Forest.*

CHAPTER II

THE SONGS IN THE PLAYS

A study of the songs in the plays reveals several reasons for Jonson's later success in combining music with dramatic incident in the masques. The songs carry forward the plot, they take the place of conversation, they emphasize emotional moments, they introduce characters. Jonson's cleverness in the use of song to further dramatic ends is apparent in the masques; but it is difficult to trace the development of his craftsmanship through the long series of elaborate court entertainments. The masques are in fact evidences of a fully developed technic rather than the work of an apprentice learning to write songs. In the plays, however, we can observe the playwright's early experiments, his first musical successes, and we may account in part, at least, for his later glories as a masque writer.

Another evidence of craftsmanship important in the production of masques, an evidence more easily traced through the plays than in the librettos of the masques, is the use of the musical talent of his actors. Jonson made songs to display the talent of a well trained voice or to cover up the deficiencies of an uncultivated singer. It may have been fortunate for the court and for Jonson that the poet could prepare an elaborate stanza suited to the vocalizing of an ambitious courtier who possessed a magnificent tenor. It was equally fortunate that Jonson could devise a song which would scarcely call attention to the fact that another great lord who enjoyed acting and dancing possessed a feeble voice. The librettos of the masques do not reveal the names of the singers, nor the nature of their voices. But we can follow Jonson's work quite easily in the plays. We know that he made elaborate polyphonic songs for the well trained companies of children, and that he made simple songs for the amateur singers of adult companies. At times he provided that a special singer be imported into the cast to interpret stanzas which were too difficult for an untrained voice. Thus, a study of the plays with particular reference to the companies which produced them, shows a distinct relationship between lyric structure and the ability of the singers. Stanzas

44

for cultivated voices contain syllables suited to trilling, vocalizing or delays. Words and phrases particularly adapted to diminuendos and crescendos govern the arrangement and length of poetic cadences. Vowels suited to tonal shading, inflections of the voice, occur and reoccur. Lines which are flexible under the stress of such vocal gymnastics are appealing when read aloud. They possess the singing quality which is so desirable in lyric verse.

Sometimes deliberately, on the other hand, Jonson abandoned the conventional means of securing lyric quality. Nano's songs, for instance, are snatches of plot dependent for their appeal upon facial expression, gesture, or comic interpretation. Jonson did not waste a haunting melody on the clown who painted his face to amuse the audience, and who very likely had no vocal talent. Nano's syllables are clear cut, easily understood, short, even choppy. They describe a patent medicine; they interpret a situation; but they are not melodically beautiful. Such stanzas are framed for the tones of ordinary conversation, rather than for singing.

SONGS FOR THE CASE IS ALTERED

" The Case is Altered was first published in 1609, being entered in the Stationer's Register on January 26th of that year." [1] " The play, had, according to the title-page of the Quarto, been played ' sundry times ' by the Children of the Blackfriars, i.e. of the Chapel," [2] so that at the time of its publication it was ten or eleven years old. Though the main body of the play was written before 1599,[3] the opening scene was added to or revised sometime in 1600.[4] Previous to the writing of this play Jonson had shown no interest in song-writing. The earlier plays contain no songs. Quite, possibly, then, Jonson originally provided no songs for The Case is Altered; but when he bargained with the manager of the Children, he may have agreed to prefix the cobbler's song to the first scene, and to insert directions for other music later in the play.

[1] *Ben Jonson, The Man and His Work,* ed. by C. H. Herford and Percy Simpson, Oxford at the Clarendon Press, 1925, Vol. I, p. 305.
[2] *Ibid.*
[3] *Ibid.,* p. 306.
[4] *Ibid.*

This problematic first scene opens with Juniper sitting at the door of his cobbler's shop, singing a stanza about doleful news. The song may take the place of a discarded prologue, though there is nothing in the context particularly pertinent to the business of the play.   More likely the verses were tacked on as an after-thought.   Onion, the second character to make his appearance, enters soon after the song begins, but Onion's interruptions do not disturb the soloist, who continues to sing:

> You woful wights, give ear a while,
> And mark the tenor of my style,
> Which shall such trembling hearts unfold,
> As seldom hath to-fore been told.
> Such chances rare, and doleful news,
>
> (Enter Onion, in haste)

Onion:	Fellow Juniper! peace a God's name.
Jun.:	As may attempts your wits to muse.
On.:	Od's so, hear man! a pox on you!
Jun.:	And cause such trickling ears to pass,
	Except your hearts be flint, or brass,
On.:	Juniper! Juniper!
Jun.:	To hear the news which I shall tell,
	That in Castella once befel,—

Although Jonson has couched the song in the popular ballad lingo of the time, there is a restraint and a reticence about the melody which suggests that Jonson could not fully give himself up to the popular ballad tunes.   The song may have been sung to the old tune, *The Children in the Wood,* which Chappell published in his *Popular Music of the Olden Time.*[5]   Richard Brome apparently used the same tune for his song beginning " Now ponder well," in the *Jovial Crew.*   The stanza shows evidences of song tendencies popular with the Elizabethan composers, such as irregular line lengths, the suggestion of dialogue, (though part of the conversation is not assigned to a singing voice) and the use of words which could be dramatically interpreted, *woful, doleful* and *trembling.*

On the whole, however, the song is not the product of a skilled craftsman.   The meaning of the lines has little to do with the action of the play.   The words are merely words, filling in spaces —mere syllables corresponding to musical phrases.   The song

[5] *Op. cit.,* p. 201.

lacks the exquisite harmony between words and notes of *Drink to me only with thine eyes;* it lacks the delicate seriousness, the artless art of the better known lyric. Yet it does not show the freedom from set form that *Follow a shadow* reveals. There are evidences of technical ability, but these evidences are forerunners of the elaborate patterns which Jonson later devised for the masque songs—when he used choral interpretations of slight actions, and antiphonal dialogue instead of conversation.

There are indications that other songs occurred in the play but for some reason Jonson did not publish the words for them. Possibly he expected the children to supply their own songs (for the small actors probably possessed a large repertoire). Or in later years Jonson may have been ashamed of his youthful efforts and purposely excluded the words.

The text calls for music in Act III, Sc. 1, when Angelo withdraws from the stage singing *tau dery dery.* The phrase is a meaningless outburst enabling Angelo to make a debonair exit. Possibly the words *tau dery dery* were set to an elaborate harmony like the fa-la-la songs discussed in the last chapter (page 30). Whatever the circumstances may have been, apparently Jonson shirked all responsibility for the words of the song.

The directions again call for music at the beginning of Act IV, Sc. 3. This time Juniper is discovered at the door of his shop singing. But we do not know how long or what he sang. Just as in Scene 1 of Act 1 Onion breaks into the performance imploring the cobbler to stop:

"Fellow Juniper, no more of thy songs and sonnets; sweet Juniper, no more of thy hymns and madrigals; thou singest, but I sigh." It is interesting to note that Onion does not distinguish between solos and part-songs but uses a variety of terms to describe Juniper's melody. This is an excellent illustration of the Elizabethan use of musical terms.[7]

On the whole, *The Case is Altered* is not a very satisfactory combination of song and drama. Jonson was either indifferent to the value of music, or not interested in assuming responsibility for the words of the songs.

[7] See Chapter I, page 16.

The Songs in Cynthia's Revels

Having established relations with the manager of the Children, Jonson awakened to the fact that music could be extensively employed in plays for the small actors. Perhaps the problems which arose in the production of the *Case is Altered* convinced him that it would be well to learn to use songs to some better purpose. Perhaps the manager of the Children insisted. At any rate, Jonson began to court the muse of song. He courted with fervor. In 1601, he wrote *Cynthia's Revels,* a play which was largely a frame work filled with songs. The play exists for the songs, each of which is a pure lyric, not a scrap of the plot set to music. In the masques, as well as in the later plays, the characters come in singing, or go off the stage singing, or group themselves conveniently in order that song may be a natural expression of their action. But in *Cynthia's Revels,* song is foremost and the dialogue and situations leading up to the music exist for the sake of the songs.

The first song in *Cynthia's Revels* is a very beautiful canzonet. The setting calls for three voices.[8] Unfortunately, there is only one person on the stage qualified to sing it, so Jonson arranged for Mercury to summon voices out of the air to assist the lone Dryad. This solitary nymph, Echo, has just risen from a fountain and begs to celebrate the memory of her dead lover, Narcissus, in tuneful ritual. The fountain disappears after the first scene, and is of no further importance aside from lending its name to the play. The funeral celebration is gratuitous as far as the plot is concerned. But the fountain story, and the funeral, serve to introduce the song, and the song is well worth its labored introduction.

> Slow, slow, fresh fount, keep time with my salt tears:
> Yet slower, yet; O faintly, gentle springs:
> List to the heavy part the music bears,
> Woe weeps out her division, when she sings.
> Droop herbs and flowers,
> Fall grief in showers,
> Our beauties are not ours.

[8] Henry Youll's *Canzonets to Three Voices,* 1608. For recent notation see E. H. Fellowe's *English Madrigal School,* Volume XXVIII, Stainer and Bell, London, 1923.

> O, I could still,
> Like melting snow upon some craggy hill,
> Drop, drop, drop, drop,
> Since nature's pride is now a wither'd daffodil.[9]

Youll's setting for the song was very likely used in the production of the play; but whether or not Youll's arrangement was actually the one prepared for the performance, it serves very well to illustrate the kind of music that composers revelled in. It is the setting Jonson prepared for, and expected, and if it is not the identical notation which was employed, it must be very much like the original.

Sadness is the key-note of the song. Youll has emphasized the mood in every conceivable way. There is melancholy in the carefully delayed cadences, in the slow rhythm, in the sustained notes, and in the repetition of words suggesting dolefulness. The first word, *slow,* is taken by the treble, sustained through a measure, and immediately followed by a second word *slow.* At the repetition of the treble, the cantus secundus begins with its first *slow* in another pitch, sustaining the word throughout the measure. In the fourth measure, while the cantus secundus is still repeating *slow,* the bassus begins its first *slow* in a lower key, drawing out the dismal effect by suspensions, and repetitions, while the treble is moaning *tears* and the secundus is beginning on *tears.*

The word *slower* in the second line is emphatically drawn out through a measure, and each voice in turn holds the note set to the word *slower,* through several successive measures. "The heavy part the music bears" may refer to an obvious bass voice or to the solemn atmosphere of the piece. The treble and secundus are singing at intervals widely separated from the bass, during the third line, so that the low voice is actually heavy by contrast to the two higher parts.

> "Droop herbs and flowers,
> Fall grief and showers"

are pictorially treated. *Droop* begins on a high note and the other words are sung to successively lower tones, descending in a minor scale to the lowest note, for *flowers.* The *drops* are sim-

[9] *Cynthia's Revels,* I, 1. Compare Thomas Nabbe's use of the same meter, and to a certain extent the same idea, in his "Flow, flow delight," *Microsmus,* III.

ilarly treated.   Five *drops* follow each other down the scale, with
an extra " O, drop, drop, drop " added to conclude the falling
cadence.   The last two *drops* are drawn out and sustained for
several measures, intensifying the passivity of the motion of the
slow falling water.   " Some craggy hill " likewise receives pictorial
treatment.   From a note approximating *B* on the word *some* there
is a leap to *F* for *craggy* and a second *F* for *hill*.   The succession
from *B* to *F* is disagreeable, thus stressing the uncouth or *craggy*
imagery in the words.   The two syllables sustained on high *F* lend
an element of loftiness, suggesting the top of a hill, both in the
notation and in the vocal production.   The same words are repeated as a refrain, repeated in another discordant interval, a succession of *B* to *C* sharp.

The last line resembles a wail, a succession of notes descending
the scale.   The last note is sustained and supported by the tones
of a diminished tonic chord.

As a lyric, one of the best in Jonson's plays as well as one of
the most elaborate, the song is an extremely adequate embodiment
of grief.   It is akin to Fletcher's funeral song beginning " Come,
you whose loves are dead," [12] though it exhales a delicate sadness
which Fletcher's completely lacks.   There is infinitely greater
preparation for the composers, as well as a more evenly sustained
verbal melody, than in Daniel's " Had sorrow ever fitter place " [13]
which was the " dolefullest," most " sighingest musicke " that
could " entertain sad thoughts."   In preparing for elaborate
harmony, Jonson naturally devised words which would sound
well when repeated,—with vowels suited to vocalising.   If a word
is repeated once it engraves an impression either pleasant or
otherwise upon the ear.   If it is repeated many times, it must
be a very melodious word not to disgust the listener.   So that
in preparing *droop,* and *drop,* and *slow* and *tears,* Jonson selected
simple words, words which could be repeated without outraging
the sense.   No one objects to a repetition of the word *drop,* nor

[10] Note the predominacy of sighing, sobbing, grieving words in Shakespeare's Willow Song, Othello, IV, 3, in Fletcher's " Weep no more," *Queen
of Cor.* III. 2; in Dekkar's " Love is a sickness," *Hymen's Triumph,* and
in Rowley's " To sigh, to sob, to pine, to groan," *Nobel Soldier.*

[11] Contrast Ariel's comments on the burden of " Come unto these yellow
sands," *Tempest.*

[12] See footnote 10, Chapter II.

[13] Daniel, Samuel, *Hymen's Triumph, A Pastoral Traji-Comedy,* I, 1, 1615.

of *tears,* nor of *slow.*   In fact the mere mention of one of these
words indicates that a repetition will follow.   You expect one
drop to follow another, one tear to fall after another, and *slow*
repeated is very much like *slow* sustained.   These words which
stand the test of great frequency of repetition, are simple words,
but words connoting elaborate musical effects.

The next song in *Cynthia's Revels* contains many suggestions
for composers.   Prosaites enters (Act II, Sc. 1) followed by
two gallants, swaggers across the stage flourishing a bottle and
singing:

> Come follow me, my wags, and say as I say,
> There's no riches save in rags, hey day, dey, day;
> You that profess this art, come away, come away,
> And help to bear a part.   Hey day, hey day, etc.

The topers are off to discover the new fountain of nectar.
" Come follow me " invites the company to make an exit, and
clears the stage for the next act.   " Help to bear a part " probably signified for the rest of the actors to join in a roistering *hey
dey* chorus.   The *come away* phrase could be taken up and repeated by one part, then another, borne off by voices at varying
pitches, and varying rhythms.   *He dey* lines would presumably
be treated like *fa-la-la* choruses, and harmonized elaborately
or simply according to the fancy of the composer.   One of the
most engaging attributes of the song is its brevity.

In lyric appeal the lines resemble Shakespeare's *Jog on jog on* [16]
which was used for a similar purpose—to clear the stage.   Both
express the sentiments of the merry heart of an irresponsible way-
farer.   Fletcher stirs the same vein in his " Cast your caps and
cares away," and Brome echoes the sentiment of the second line
in his theme for the *Beggar's Opera.*   Jonson's capricious *hey
dey hey dey* measures counteract the sorrowful effect of the fountain song; the short gay lines excell in their own way quite as
effectively as the more stately refrains of the solemn lyric.   The
playwright had already discovered the expediency of an exit song
in the *tau dery dery dery* of Angelo's departing.   *Come follow me*
is something of an improvement over *tau dery dery dery* for the
context of the former conveys an idea about the occupation of
the revellers off stage, or between scenes.

In Act III, Sc. 3, Jonson uses irrelevant syllables to emphasize

[16] Winter's Tale, IV, 2.

the irrelevant speech of his mock courtiers. Asotus and Amorphus are practicing the courting of a mistress. Asotus glibly fakes the following speech and dance, interspersing his performance with the bit of song indicated:

" Say you so, sweet lady! *Lan te de de de dedant dant dant* (Sings and dances). " No in faith madame, whosoever told your ladyship so abused you."

Lan te de de de dedant, a foolish, meaningless group of syllables, rendered in falsetto voice might well become symbolic of the character of Asotus.

The next song in the play is a " melting " sugar-coated love ditty presenting yet another contrast in mood to the sorrowing fountain music, and the devil-may-care *Come Away* song. Heden accompanies himself on the lyra, an instrument which alone can " infuse soul into the most . . . dull disposed creature upon earth." [17] The tone of the song is entirely in keeping with the coxcomb who sings it.

> O, that joy so soon should waste!
>   Or so sweet a bliss
> As a kiss
> Might not forever last!
> So sugared, so melting, so soft, so delicious.
>   The dew that lies on roses,
>   Then the morn herself discloses,
>   Is not so precious.
> O rather than I would it smother,
> Were I to taste such another;
>   It should be my wishing
>   That I might die with kissing.[18]

Irregular line lengths allow for the smooth adjustment of the stanza to alternating rhythms and changes of tempo. *Might forever last* indicates a long drawn out cadence, and the word *die* was undoubtedly sustained beyond the requirements of a regular rhythm. One member of the audience declares the " long die note did aride " him most, " but it was somewhat too long." If the word *kissing* was also lengthily sustained, probably Jonson was indulging in a bit of irony at the expense of the giddy court world. The playwrights had a habit of mocking the sports of love in their songs, as Fletcher's *Take her and hug her,* and

[17] Cynthia's Revels, IV, 1.
[18] *Ibid.*

Shakespeare's *Love, Love, Nothing but Love* imply. The verbal
melody is exquisite, as one might expect from words intended
for a trained voice. The singer would need to have a good voice
to dwell leisurely on the full vowels, to glide smoothly over the
melting sibilants, and rest fondy on *wishing,* and *kissing,* and
other words potential in pictorial significance.

Noble thought there was no more delightful song in the whole
realm of our dramatic literature.[19] It compares very favorably
in verbal melody with Fletcher's *How long shall I pine for love?*
and as far as choice of subject matter is concerned is very closely
akin to *Take, Oh take those lips away.* Nearly every word could
be emphasized by tonal shading, and every cadence falls naturally
into the rise and fall of pulsating melody.

The glove song was prepared in similar vein. The gallant
who interprets it is a sentimental courtling, grieving half heartedly
over the death of the owner of the glove. The singer cares far
more for his vocalizing, for the beauty of the notes, and the manner in which he delivers the song than for the sorrow he might
be expected to express. The triviality of the emotional content,
the concern over his influence on the audience, and the technical
explanations preceding and following the performance are symbolic of Amorphus' character. He had set the words to his most
" affected instrument, the lyra," and probably accompanied himself
while singing. He married all the ascending syllables to ascending notes, and all the descending syllables to descending notes.[20]
This stanza is frequenty selected by anthologists. Like the preceding song, it is agreeably suited both to singing and to reading
aloud.

Amorphus' comments upon song-writing indicate that Jonson

[19] Noble, Richmond, *Shakespear's Use of Song,* Oxford University Press,
1923, p. 140.

[20] Amorphus' assertion that he had married all of his syllables to corresponding notes, to notes which ascended and descended, etc., indicates that
Amorphus had picked out a tune and written words which fitted the tune.
See Chapter I, p. 34 on the subject of Jonson's aptitude in arranging lines
to tunes. It was a more or less common trait of Elizabethan verse writers
to adjust words to old tunes. John Donne set three verses to " tunes which
had been made before " . . . and Herrick also is reported to have made
words for tunes which were popular at the time of his writing. For a
discussion of this practice among dramatists, see the *Notes* to Edward
Bliss Reed's *Songs from the British Drama,* Yale University Press, New
Haven, 1925.

by this time was fully conscious of the technical aspects of his art. From the production of the *Poetaster* on, Jonson's songs were by no means accidental in their attractiveness to composers.

Also, Jonson was conscious that his song was a very good poem to read aloud. Very likely he did not wish the audience to miss the beauty of his songs as spoken lyrics. Consequently Amorphus reads the verse aloud previous to singing it, in very much the same way that the English Singers today read aloud before they sing.

The next song is well known for its poetic beauty: *Queen and Huntress, Chaste and Fair*.[21] Hesperus is introduced into the play for the sole purpose, apparently, of singing this one song. Youll's setting as a canzonet was probably not used in the play unless voices from the air or from some unknown quarter assisted Hesperus. (As in the Fountain song.) Jonson's directions call for "Music accompanied, Hesperus sings." Jonson may have meant *accompanied by other voices,* not by instruments, but the meaning is doubtful. As far as the stanzaic structure is concerned, the poem is not definitely adapted to any one type of musical setting. It could be arranged equally well as canzonet, harmonic part song, or solo. The refrain suggests the Ferraboscan habit of repeating the last line twice at the close of a solo.[22] The division of the first line into easily repeated words, or phrases, indicates polyphonic setting. Undoubtedly the song is a good song, and Youll's setting,[22a] whether used in the play or not, proves that it attracted the interest of a contemporary musician.

The concluding song of the play is an effective palinode. The words sum up the entire action, and interpret the allegory. The dialogue song was popular with singers and composers, giving the separate characters opportunity to display their several abili-

[21] Compare Jonson's hymn with Fletcher's "Song to Cynthia," *Maid's Tragedy,* I, 1.

[22] The following songs, which were set to music by Ferrabosco (written by Ben Jonson) repeat the last line: *Come my Celia, If all the Cupids, It was no policy of court, Yes, were the loves or false or straying, So Beauty on the waters stood,* and others, from Alphonso Ferrabosco's *Book of Ayres.* See also Shakespeare's *Ant. Cleop.,* II, 1, for repetition of the last line in the song beginning "Come thou Monarch."

[22a] Because Henry Youll arranged other music for this play, it is believed he arranged the music for this song. It is not, however, contained in the volume of canzonets already referred to in foot-note 8, p. 48.

ties, with choral flourish as climax. Cynthia and her nymphs, Amorphus and the courtiers, make their exits in pairs, singing their good new intentions as they depart. Amorphus and Phantaste alternate in the dialogue measures, while the chorus swells the refrain " Good Mercury defend us." [23] Crites and Mercury chime in with a final moral:

Palinode

Amor: From Spanish shrugs, French faces, smirks, irpes and
        all affected humours,
Chor.: Good Mercury defend us.
Phant.: From secret friends, sweet servants, loves, doves, and
        such fantastic humours,
Chorus: Good Mercury defend us . . . etc. . . .

The song continues cataloguing the follies of the court, with the choral chant until Mercury and Crites conclude:

> Now each one dry his weeping eyes,
> And to the Well of Knowledge haste;
> Where, purged of your maladies,
> You may of sweeter waters taste:
> And with refined voice report
> The grace of Cynthia, and her court.

The emotional appeal of this song is too closely linked with the content of the play to be universal. Elizabethans who were familiar with the ways of the court may have found this song stirring as well as satisfying to their emotions. Without doubt the song draws together the straying threads of plot, and serves a much needed function, that of bringing the cast together for a concluding spectacle. It is too distinctly a part of Elizabethan life for modern readers to judge as a song or as a lyric. If we could hear the enthusiastic courtiers shouting forth their high resolves, with the mockingly solemn refrain, if we could feel with the audience a due amount of disgust at the foppish manners of the gallant, and sympathize with the well meaning Crites, we might be qualified to pass judgment on the performance. It leaves the reader with a sense of definite finality, with no doubt as to the meaning of the play, and music ringing in his ears. This palinode is a forerunner of the elaborate choral conclusions to the masques, which, in later years Jonson learned to use with unrivalled success.

[23] For similar song structure see Lyly's *Endymion*, IV, 3, " Pinch him, pinch him," and *Galatea*, I, 4, the song beginning " Rocks and shelves and seas;" *Gal.* IV, 2, " O Yes, O Yes."

Songs from the Poetaster

By the time Jonson had finished *Cynthia's Revels* he had learned to make songs of many patterns. He had tried his hand at part songs, and solos, choruses and dialogues. The *Poetaster* is more or less of a continuation of the song-writing which Jonson practiced in the former play. The characters belong to the same caste of superficial courtier, and they sing the same kind of superficial songs. And Jonson himself still in the hey dey of young manhood penned many a gallant love-ditty for the *Poetaster*.

The first incident related to music in this play is the humorous skit mentioned in the Introduction to this study, pp. 6, 7. A group of courtiers and fashionable gallants have gathered for a feast, and in order to speed the time before the banquet is served they urge one of their number, Hermogenes, a musician, to sing to them. Hermogenes wishes to be coaxed, and he refuses. To encourage the musician, Crispinus, another member of the group, begins to sing a dainty lyric descriptive of his mistress.

> If I freely may discover
> What may please me in my lover,
> I would have her fair and witty,
> Savouring more of court than city;
> A little proud, but full of pity;
> Light and humorous in her toying,
> Oft building hopes, and soon destroying,
> Long, but sweet in the enjoying;
> Neither too easy nor too hard;
> All extremes I would have barred.[25]

The company applaud Crispinus, and the praise arouses Hermogenes' envy. Crispinus had sung a stanza of Hermogenes' composition, and Hermogenes cannot long remain in silence. When he had once begun to sing, he was greatly encouraged by the sound of his own voice, and could not be entreated to stop. " 'Tis the common disease of all these musicians," said Julia, " they know no mean, to be entreated either to begin or end." The incident closes when the gentlemen lead the ladies to the banqueting hall, all of them hastening to make their exit before Hermogenes can sing " yet another." Hermogenes' song was a continuation of Crispinus' stanza, both stanzas being written in the same meter, and probably both were sung to the same tune.

[25] II, 1.

Hermogenes sings:

> She should be allow'd her passions,
> So they were but used as fashions;
> Sometimes froward, and then frowning
> Sometimes sickish, and then swowning,
> Every fit with change still crowning.
> Purely jealous I would have her
> Then only constant when I crave her;
> 'Tis a virtue should not save her.
> Thus, not her delicates would cloy me,
> Neither her peevishness annoy me.

The music for "If I freely may discover" is an elaborate air, by an unknown composer. Mr. Lindsay thinks the manuscript dates between 1615 and 1636.[26]   His analysis of the setting is as follows: "The melody is simple, adhering consistently to major tonality. The key is F major. The air is pitched for low voice, requiring a range of an octave, C to c.   The outstanding features of this air are:

1. Irregularity of Form.
2. Variety of Rhythm.
3. Syllable accentuation by
    a. Position on strong beats.
    b. Position on long notes.
    c. Position on syncopated notes.
4. Complexity of melody.
5. Narrow range, usually a ninth.
6. Authentic harmony, indicated by air and bass.
7. A small amount of real counterpoint written down, and probably more indicated.[27]

The mood of the tune is light and graceful, suitably adapted to the theme of the verse.   The first rhyming words, *discover*, and *lover*, are emphasized by bringing the two first lines to rest upon the same tone.   At the close of the line, "I would have her faire and witty," there is a turn so that the word *witty* corresponds to a leap from E to A.   This breaks the word into two syllables *wit-ty* so that the "t" sound is emphasized—the staccato effect

---

[26] The manuscript of the music is in the British Museum, Add. 24665. Mr. Lindsay's discussion of this song is in manuscript, *Music on the Elizabethan Stage,* Library of the University of North Carolina, Chapel Hill.

[27] The discussion here mentioned is an interesting analysis of the music for this song. I have quoted as much as pertains to this study, from pages 75, 76, 77.

bringing a light gayety into the measure. The line " Light and
amorous in her toying " corresponds to a change of the rhythm,
giving an effect of leisure, of slightly slower tempo, dalliance,
with the word "toying" set to a drawn out gliding turn. " De-
stroying " is set to a similar turn, and also " enjoying " carries
out the symmetry of the musical pattern with a like cadence ending. The word " Long " is set to a whole note, and the following
" sweet " to a dotted half, so that the effect of the phrase is again
that of leisurely graceful motion. The last line, in which the
composer added the word " but " to the beginning, is arranged
to a tune with neither high nor low notes, so that the even and
gradual descent to tonic carries out the significance of the words.

Hermogenes says that he himself had composed the two stanzas
just quoted; but the next song in the play was composed and
sung by Crispinus.[28]

The theme of this third song is light,[29] the lines are of irregular
lengths, and the cadences short and well suited to polyphonic
setting. *Wanton, waileth,* and *plucked* call for pictorial treatment.
Wanton has been discussed in this connection (Chapter I, p. 32).
Waileth suggests a series of long, full minor tones; and *plucked*
might be emphasized by the plucking of strings. Crispinus accompanied his song on the viol:

> Love is blind, and a wanton;
> In the whole world, there is scant one
>   —Such another;
>   No, not his mother.
> He hath pluck'd her doves and sparrows,
> To feather his sharp arrows,
>   And alone prevaileth,
>   While sick Venus waileth.
> But if Cypris once recover
>   The wag, it shall behove her
>   To look better to him;
>   Or she will undo him.

Master Albius' comment at the close of the song carries with
it a note of Jonson's scorn for the courtier's admiration of this

[28] Act IV, Sc. 1.

[29] The same theme occurs in Fletcher's " Merciless Love, whom nature
hath night " *The Chances,* II, 2. Fletcher's song requires a lute accompaniment and is sung off stage. The lines are longer, less irregular, and
less melodious.

sort of popular love lyric, scorn expressed in the choice of words which Albius uses: "O most odoriferous music!"

The revelling songs in Act IV, Sc. 1 suggest none of the mirth and care-free love of the flowing bowl which one might expect from the chief lord of the Mermaid. These stanzas reveal an appreciation of pleasure, not an actual participation in it.[30] The masquerading gallants have arrived at a feast, and are waiting for entertainment.   The situation is somewhat dull until Gallus shouts for music to stir up his companions:

> Wake! our mirth begins to die;
>   Quicken it with tunes and wine.
> Raise your notes; you're out, fie, fie!
>   This drowsiness is an ill sign.
>   We banish him the quire of gods,
>   That droops agen;
>   Then all are men,
> For here's not one but nods.

The short irregular lines would offer a composer many chances for changes in rhythm, and many dividing points for polyphonic

[30] Johnson who was noted as leader of the revellers at the Mermaid and at the Apollo has left us scarcely a revelling song worthy of the name unless it be *Drink to me only with thine eyes,* which suggests the love theme more than drinking and revelling themes. Jonson's servant, however, Richard Brome, wrote more drinking songs for his *Jovial Crew* than Jonson included in all of his works. One is tempted to accuse Brome of having stored up Jonson's songs of merry-making and of putting them to good use. It certainly appears from the numbers of drinking songs that master and servant left to posterity, that Brome, not Jonson, was the great Elizabethan worshipper of Bacchus.

The Elizabethan dramatists, were on the whole given to including drinking songs in their plays. Fletcher's "Let the bells ring," a three men's song in Act III, Sc. 2, of the *Spanish Curate* is a rollicking verse. "God Lyaeus ever young," *Valentian,* V, 8, shows Fletcher's more stately mode of expressing worship for the wine God. Shakespeare's "And let me the cannikin clink, clink" *Othello,* II, reveals Shakespeare's ability to make a light drinking song, *Ant. Cleop.,* II, 7, while his "Come thou Monarch of the Vine" invokes a lofty respect for Bacchus akin to the Jonsonian measures above quoted. Chapman uses but one song in all of his plays, an eight-line drinking song with a refrain, in the *Blind Beggars of Alexandria.* Drinking songs might be divided into two classes, the popular type belonging to the taverns, and the more stately echo of the old Dionysian revels. Jonson may have been so conscious of the origin and purpose of drinking songs that he would not allow himself to be known as the author of the popular jingling measures of Elizabethan alehouse verse.

repetitions. The word *quicken* could be set to a flight of grace
notes; *raise* could be adapted to an ascending scale, and *droops*
to a descending scale. *Wake* deserves a crashing chord.

Fie fie [31] suggests an extemporaneous devising of a chorus
similar to the *fa-la-la* choruses mentioned in Chapter I. The
song was but weakly performed (the singers were children) so
that Jonson planned a second song for several voices, which he
designated should be sung in *louder* fashion.

The lines of this louder song contain sensuous imagery.[32]   An
audience might easily catch and understand the meaning for one
term leads or hints at another, and all the terms contribute to but
one effect, which the composer could emphasize in the musical
setting—a langorous rhythm rising to a crescendo effect in the
first line with a loud extolling of beauty. Appropriate to a revelling scene are the references to sweet odours, nectar and soft
beauty. *Lofty strain* implies that the first line was perhaps the
theme of the melody. The answer which was taken by another
voice was a variation of the main theme and there is an implica-
tion that still more singers were joining in, as accompaniment.
In this song, as in songs previously alluded to, it is impossible
to tell whether Jonson intended instrumental or vocal accompaniment. The song maintains the dialogue form throughout:

Herm.   Then, in a free and lofty strain
               Our broken tunes, we thus repair;
Cris.   And we answer them again,

[31] The *fie fie* refrain was very popular among Elizabethan dramatists
because it included a sense of ridicule, perhaps scorn, so that actors could
interpret the idea by means of facial expression, gesture, or movements
expressing scorn. Anthony Munday uses the phrase in "You stole my
love, fie upon ye fie," *John a Kent,* III. At the close of this song the
actors go into a castle singing as they make their exit, probably pointing
back with scornful gestures as they repeat "Fie upon ye fie." Fletcher
also uses the refrain in "How long shall I pine for love?" *The Maid in
the Mill,* V, 2.

[32] See Lyly's use of sensuous imagery in his "Oh for a bowl of fat
canary," written for three parts and chorus, *Alexander and, Campaspe,*
I, 3. In *Sapho and Phao,* II, 3, Lyly again uses a three man's song beginning "Merry Knaves are we not three-a?" These songs are popular
in tone, and not closely related to Jonson's more intellectual interpretation
of merriment. Fletcher's *Bonduca* opens the fourth act with a dialogue
song, also revelling in tone, and Shakespeare expresses a similarly light
theme in "Get you hence," *Winter's Tale* IV, 3.

Running division on the panting air;[33]
Ambo.:   To celebrate this feast of sense,
              As free from scandal as offence.
Herm.:   Here is beauty for the eye;
Cris.:   For the ear sweet melody.
Herm.:   Ambrosiac odors, for the smell;
Cris.:   Delicious nectar, for the taste;
Ambo.:   For the touch, a lady's waist;
              Which doth the rest excell.[34]

All of the songs from the *Poetaster* have been selected by critics
and editors for collections of lyric verse.   They are good poems
to read aloud.   Like the songs in *Cynthia's Revels,* they are composed of words which bear the test of vocalizing, of displaying
the delicate intonations of a well trained voice.   Almost every
word in every song could be repeated or sustained by a singer
who was desirous of showing off technical ability.   This, after all,
was just the sort of thing the manager of the Children's Companies wanted.   And this was the sort of thing that taught Jonson
how to select words which were suited to vocal melody.   Sometimes the words were repeated by several voices in part-song, and
tested by the severe trial of repetition for emphasis; sometimes
they were interpreted by a soloist to demonstrate breath control
and tonal shading.

And now that Jonson had fully learned his lesson in writing
songs for dramatic purposes, the Queen interrupted his career
with a command to write a masque.   Jonson had shown himself
capable of writing dramatic musical entertainments in *Cynthia's
Revels* and the *Poetaster,* and it was but natural that he should
be rewarded.   From the time of constructing his first masque,
(the Masque of Blackness 1605), the story of Jonson's use of
music to further dramatic purposes must be told in two parts:
the story of masque-writing, and the story of play-writing.   In
this chapter we will continue to trace Jonson's use of song in
his plays, though after 1605 Jonson was no longer interested in
making a play serve merely as the framework for a collection of
songs.   Much of his lyric ability was expended on the masques.

[33] Shakespeare uses this figure of speech in Romeo and Juliet, III, 5.
" Some say the lark makes sweet divisions."
[34] IV, 3.

The Music for Volpone

Jonson began the writing of *Volpone* with a practised hand. He had learned something about the use of song in the drama in his experiments with the Childrens' Companies. He had again courted the sister Muses in the *Masque of Blackness,* produced the preceding year. The songs in *Volpone* perform definite functions. They show economy of effort, and great dramatic craftsmanship.

The first song in the play is a duet beginning:

> Fools, they are the only nation,
> Worth men's envy and admiration.[35]

Volpone's two servants, Nano and Castrone, sing the song to amuse their master with the philosophy and offices of fools. Like the revelling songs in the *Poetaster* the mirth is somewhat forced. There is an absence of light, staccato consonant sounds, and a preponderance of heavy vowel sounds. The *he, he, he* of the last line cannot break the monotony of the sixteen solid preceding lines. The success of the song depends entirely upon the facial expressions, gestures, and dramatic ability of the fool and the dwarf. Probably Nano and Castrone were poor singers, but excellent actors, and Jonson prepared their parts to emphasize their peculiar abilities. The lines which they sing tell us how their faces were painted to beget laughter, and also that their buffoonery at its worst is superior to the rascality of Volpone.

This song makes its primary appeal to the intellect; it is narrative and expository, not emotional. The lines are solid, of even length, and are not suggestive of verbal melody, to say nothing of musical cadences. It is even possible that Nano and Castrone sang in discord, as a part of their clownishness, or that they pretended to improvise their words and notes, or that they sang without any tunes whatsoever.

In Nano's next song he mounts a pulpit in the street with Volpone, and attracts a crowd to hear his singing. The stanza describes a new ointment powerful enough to cure all ills. It is an enumeration of the miraculous qualities of the medicine. Nano's performance is convincing in its way, for it lures the citizens from their daily tasks and exposes them to Volpone's jests.

[35] I, 1. Compare Randolph's song beginning "Slaves are they that heap up mountains." Thomas Randolph, *Aristippus.*

Had old Hippocrates, or Galen,
That to their books put med'cines all in,
But known this secret, they had never
(Of which they will be guilty ever)
Been murderers of so much paper,
Or wasted many a hurtless taper;
No Indian drug had e'er been famed,
Tobacco, sassafras not named;
Ne yet of guacum one small stick, sir,
Nor Raymund Lully's great elixir.
Ne had been known the Danish Gonswart,
Or Paracelsus with his long sword.[37]

While a history of medecine jumbled into a song, along with such narrative and expository details as Nano chose to include, could scarcely form a melodic lyric, there have been beautiful songs written upon kindred themes.   Shakespeare's " Will you buy any tape or lace for your cape? " or " Lawn as white as driven snow " show us that propaganda songs were not destined to be without lyric appeal. Fletcher's *Broom song* is another example of a propaganda lyric; but Fletcher and Shakespeare were writing their stanzas to appeal as songs, not merely to convey information and to amuse. Observe the song devices which Fletcher employed,—the repetition of the word *broom*, the division of the lines into regular cadence lengths, the possibilities for pictorial treatment in *little, boot, kiss, bonny*, and *wars*. The alliterative appeal of the letter *b* supplied an effect of euphony lacking in Nano's song.

Broom, broom the bonny broom!
Come, buy my birchen broom!
I' the wars we have no more room
Buy all my bonny brooms!
For a kiss take two;
If those will not do,
For a little, little pleasure,
Take all my whole treasure:
If all these will not do't,
Take the broom man to boot.
Broom, broom the bonny broom!

[37] II, 1.   In the *Knight of the Burning Pestle,* II, 1, there is a song analyzing medical treatments and cures, and physical ailments, which is lighter and more song-like in quality, " 'Tis mirth that fills the veins with blood, etc."   There is a rhythmic feeling of motion and merriment in Fletcher's song which is lacking in the fool's song.

Nano's song undoubtedly reveals a cleverness on Jonson's part. He knew the secrets and the devices which contribute to song melody, yet purposely prepared it without lyric appeal. Fortunately not all of the lyrics in *Volpone* were arranged for Nano's interpretations.

The last song which Nano sings is similar to those just mentioned. It is very long and narrative and expository in nature. The accompaniment could be but an incidental addition, if there was any accompaniment.

Come, my Celia is a pleasant change from the dwarf's songs. It was set to music by Ferrabosco, and included in his *Book of Ayres*.[38] Dramatically the song is of great value. Volpone has been masquerading as a sick old man about to die. When he leaps from his couch and throws off his disguise it takes a little time to convince Celia that he means to court her. The sudden change in Volpone's character is unconvincing until he bursts forth in a fervent melody. The theme, age-old, has always been popular with musicians.

The notes provide for a great deal of musical and dramatic interpretation. The vowel sounds are oddly emphasized, and some of the runs stress syllables which are of no great importance. The word *good* is set to a descending flight of quarter and eighth notes, so that a singer would need to have perfect breath control, as well as delicate tone-shading to perform this part of the song gracefully. The word *perpetual* is divided so that the first syllable falls on two eighth notes, the second, *pet,* is held through a flight of descending tones with a turn at the end; and *u* is set to a single quarter note with *al* held for the value of a half note. The word *rise* corresponds to a lifting of the tune, from *D* to *C*. Nearly all the round full vowels are set to half notes, so that the singer could exert his best efforts at tone shading. The last two lines are repeated. The song would be performed lingeringly, with great emphasis upon the vowel sounds set to half notes. Sung by a strong male voice, with dramatic vigor, the song should be very effective in the scene. The length of the song, and slow tempo suggests deliberation, leisurely wooing. This gives the audience, as well as Celia, time to consider Volpone in his new role of suitor. It emphasizes his facility in all forms of rascality.

[38] *Book of Ayres*, Alphonso Ferrabosco, *op. cit.,* VI.

Come, my Celia, let us prove,
While we can, the sports of love,
Time will not be ours forever,
He, at length, our good will sever;
Spend not then his gifts in vain;
Suns that set may rise again;
But if once we lose this light,
'Tis with us perpetual night.
Why should we defer our joys?
Fame and rumour are but toys.
Cannot we delude the eyes
Of a few poor household spies?
Or his easier ears beguile,
Thus removed by our wile?
'Tis no sin love's fruits to steal;
But the sweet thefts to reveal;
To be taken, to be seen,
These have crimes accounted been.[39]

The poem has frequently been praised as a lyric; Jonson himself valued its literary qualities, for he chose to reprint it among his miscellaneous poems. It has great verbal melody when read aloud, and undoubtedly pleased both the poet, and the composer. Ferrabosco chose this song as one of nine of Jonson's songs to print in his collection of *Ayres*. Considering the many songs that Ferrabosco set for Jonson, we have to conclude that *Come my Celia* ranked high in Ferrabosco's opinion. (The other songs in the *Ayres* were all chosen from the masques.)

An interesting question in connection with this song is: Who sang the stanza? According to the text, Volpone himself sang his wooing song. It is possible that the actor who played Volpone was also a musician, but few adult actors were also trained singers. It is more probable that a musician back-stage sang the words, and that Volpone merely gestured with his lips.

[39] *Volpone*, III, 5. See William Cartwright's love song (sung by a boy), beginning in similar fashion, "Come my sweet, while's every strain," *The Royal Slave*, II, 3, and Fletcher's vulgar wooing song in *A Wit Without Money*, V, 5. Though dramatically these wooing songs serve primarily the same purpose, it is interesting to see how differently each dramatist has embodied the theme, and presented it in the action of a play. The Jonsonian version is based upon Catullus. Burney, in his *History of Music*, Volume III, p. 354, cites this song as an example of one of the best illustrations of the style of settings made by the greatest composers of the early seventeenth century.

THE SONGS IN EPICŒNE

At the time of the production of this play, the Children's companies were losing their popularity. The child actors who had been at their prime of youthful singing when *Cynthia's Revels* had been produced were half grown adolescents. Their voices had changed, and many of them had joined adult companies. Poets no longer planned their plays for the young actors, and very likely Jonson did not intend *Epicœne* for their use. Whatever the situation was in regard to Jonson's foreknowledge as to the company which would produce *Epicœne,* he knew that he could not depend upon actors who were also good singers. Consequently, he provided that a page should be introduced to sing the one song in the play. The introduction of the page is slightly awkward because one might expect Clerimont to sing the stanzas; but it was the custom for fashionable gallants to keep musicians in their employ, so that Jonson was faithful to the life of the times in thus introducing Clerimont's page to sing the song.

At the time of writing this play, Jonson had just finished the *Masque of Queens,* and had very likely begun *Prince Henry's Barriers.* Probably he could make use of all the good lyrics he had in store in the masques, and he did not care to squander them upon the harsh voices of the Children or upon badly trained adults. The one song in *Epicœne* shows us that Jonson was writing beautiful lyrics, and that his restricted use of musicians rather than a lack of ability must have prevented his preparation of a greater number of songs for his plays.

Still to be neat, still to be dressed is a pretty little exposition of the character and habits of Lady Haughty. Clerimont had been kept waiting in the Lady's reception room longer than his patience could endure. He imagined various excuses for her delay. She might be painting her cheeks, perfuming her hair, oiling her lips, and " piecing out her beauty as best she could." Eventually his complaining found vent in the expression of this dainty lyric, its daintiness perhaps accentuated in the performance by the tones of the childish voice of the page:

> Still to be neat, still to be drest,
> As if you were going to a feast:
> Still to be powder'd, still perfum'd,
> Lady, it is to be presumed,
> Though art's hid causes are not found,
> All is not sweet, all is not sound.

Give me a look, give me a face,
That makes simplicity a grace;
Robes loosely flowing, hairs as free;
Such sweet neglect more taketh me,
Than all the adulteries of art:
They please my eye, but not my heart.[40]

The music for these words was published in John Playford's *Collection of Select Ayres and Dialogues* in 1669. The tune is petulantly gay and debonair. The notation strictly emphasizes the mood and the meaning of the words.

There is an interesting illustration of a change in rhythm in this song. *As you were going to a feast* is set to notes stressing the syllables *go* and *to* and *feast,* whereas the lines preceding and following are set to fairly regular rhythm similar to six-eight time. The effect of this change of stress is like a labored climbing up a hill, the line moves forward, and stops, moves forward, and rests. The pitch of the tune rises slowly in much the same way, from *F* on *As* to *C* on *Feast.* The motion of *going* is also apparent in the feeling of the line. The word *go* corresponds to a dotted quarter note, and the *ing* ending is set to an eighth of the same pitch. *Feast* is tied to a half note, implying that the tune has arrived at a definite pausing place; there is a sense of triumph at the sound of this long drawn out C,—triumph in having mounted thus far to earn the right to rest.

The four musical phrases beginning with the first word *still* are set to variations of the same theme. Each *still* begins a phrase one tone higher than the preceding *still,* so that there is a sense of increasing achievement at each repetition. These musical phrases are enough alike to suggest symmetry, and different enough for pleasing variation. The beginning of the last line of the first stanza, *All is not sweet,* is repeated, with the second *All* corresponding to a tone a pitch lower than the first

[40] I, 1. Richard Brome wove the same theme into a song beginning "Let not the corrupted steame," *The Novella,* III, 1. Brome apparently tried to defend the ladies who used artificial coloring. His answer to Jonson's "wherefor paint?" is that as old age approaches, ladies may yet appear youthful and winsome if they are skilled in the methods of applying artificial coloring, etc. Jonson's poem, as well as Herrick's "Delight in Disorder," was based on Martial's fifty-eighth epigram. (For a discussion of these two poems see F. W. Moorman's *Biographical and Critical Study of Robert Herrick,* New York, John Lane and Co., 1910, p. 232.)

All. The notation for *All is not sound* is of similar construction to the two phrases just mentioned. The third *all* starts a new musical phrase a tone yet lower than the second *all.* Variation occurs in the last cadence by a turn of grace notes on the word *is,* causing a short delay, and adding a touch of expectancy before the final satisfying *sound.*

Jonson's use of song devices is particularly apparent in the repetition of the word *still. Still, still, still* is comparable to *drop, drop, drop* in establishing a mood of expectancy.

Playford's choice of this song for his song-book indicates that the lyric was still popular fifty years after its composition. Later editors and critics have praised it, and on the whole the song seems to have pleased Lady Haughty herself for she ceased her prinking and came to join Clerimont.

The Songs for Bartholomew Fair, 1614

Nightingale is the chief musician in *Bartholomew Fair,* in fact the most outstanding musician in any of Jonson's plays. He is the only professional musician among Jonson's characters, professional in the sense that he claimed to earn his living by selling songs. In reality, perhaps he was more of a scamp and scalawag than a singer, and he earned more money cutting purses than by singing songs. But he is a musician of a kind and the music lesson he administers to Cokes is not without value to our study.

When the Fair is first opening, Ursula the pig woman is preparing her booth; Leatherhead is shouting *rattles, halberts, horses, fiddles;* and Nightingale suddenly interrupts the ginger bread crier, and all of the other Fair activities by a demonstration of his own merchandise:

> Now the Fair's afilling!
> O, for a tune to startle
> The birds o' the booths here billing,
> Yearly with old saint Bartle!
> The drunkards they are wading,
> The punks and chapmen trading;
> Who'd see the Fair without his lading?
> Buy any ballads, new ballads?

The subject matter of the song rises so naturally from the action on the stage, that if the words were not jingling in song fashion, it would be difficult to know whether they were sung or shouted. Jonson's direction *sings* helps to allay the doubt. Nightingale claimed that his ballads were charms which could prevent the evils likely to befall a wanderer in the Fair. Consequently the stanzas contain weird imagery calculated to draw one's attention to godly garters, a dragon's heart, Saint George, or the devil.

Coke's music lesson is amusing, and at the same time an integral part of the plot. Cokes was a simple knave whose mad passion, for the moment, was to learn to sing. He hailed Nightingale, and pleaded for a lesson. Meanwhile Nightingale and Cutpurse had plotted to rob the silly boy so that Coke's salutation proved an introduction to the kind of meeting they desired. Nightingale first sings to Cokes, then Cokes tries to memorize the stanzas by rote. His stupidity is amusing because the words of the song warn him to beware of a Cutpurse, and we can see that he is being robbed even while he is practicing the refrain. Probably Cokes' wretched attempts at singing proved humorous to a musically sophisticated Elizabethan audience. Nightingale sang several stanzas but Cokes never succeeded in imitating more than a line or two of the refrain. The following is an example of a stanza of Nightingale's ballad:

> My masters, and friends, and good people, draw near,
> And look, to your purses, for that I do say;
> And though little money in them you do bear
> It costs more to get, than to lose in a day.
> You oft have been told,
> Both the young and the old
> And bidden beware of the cutpurse so bold.
> Then if you heed not, free me from the curse,
> Who both give you warning, for, and the cut-purse.
> Refrain:
> Youth, youth, thou hadst better been starved by thy nurse
> Than live to be hanged for cutting a purse.[41]

In this song, Jonson amuses us, makes us laugh, and sometimes makes us think, but he does not stir our feelings. The lines are a jingling kind of melody, appropriate for a popular type of street ballad with an appeal of their own. They do not rouse our emotions nor satisfy a longing for beauty. They fulfill

---

[41] III, 1. This song was probably sung to the tune of *Paddington's Pound*, which is discussed and printed in Chappel's *Popular Music of the Olden Time*, Vol. I, p. 123.

Jonson's dramatic need at a definite time in a play, they carry forward the plot by emphasizing Cokes' stupidity, and Nightingale's cleverness.

THE MUSIC FOR THE DEVIL IS AN ASS, 1616

After the year 1616, Jonson's ability to write plays began to decline. However, the King, now and then requested a masque and Jonson tended more and more to focus his interest on court entertainment. This shifting of interest from stage to palace may account for the play-wright's neglect of lyrics in his later plays. For though he continued to make elaborate songs for the masques, he used very few songs in his plays. The few songs which he occasionally inserted in a play, however, show that at this time Jonson was a master of song-writing.

Have you seen but a bright lily grow? is one of the loveliest of all of Jonson's lyrics. At the beginning of Act II, Sc. 2, Wittipol persuades his friend Manly (a musician imported to sing the song?) to sing certain verses "unto a tune" he "loved so well." The words for this first song are not included in the text. But Manly's song attracts Mrs. Fitzdotterel to a nearby window. At her appearance, Manly leaves the stage, Wittipol breaks into rhapsodies over his mistress' beauty, and eventually sings the caressing love-lyric, *Have you seen but a bright lily grow?*

The fact that Manly sings the first song would indicate that he was the better singer of the two, and that he made an exit, perhaps to sing the second song back-stage, leaving Wittipol to pose as the soloist. Although but one stanza of the song was directly set to music, Jonson printed two stanzas in the play, and three stanzas in his *Underwoods* collection. The first song, which Manly sang on the stage, may have been one of the stanzas printed in the *Underwoods*.

Of these three stanzas, the last is the obvious one to attract a composer. The lines glide along smoothly with frequent repetitions of liquid sounds. Alliteration and a repetition of full round vowel sounds also contribute fluidity to the melody. A long drawn out "O" sound recurs emphatically in the rhyme-endings, reminiscent of the leisurely drawn out "O" sounds in *Slow, slow, fresh fount*. In the last line of the stanza, seven "O" sounds alternate with seven "S" sounds resulting in a strange rhythmic delay, smooth gliding, yet softly vibrant.

The musical arrangement [42] of the stanza shows that the composer emphasized and elaborated upon the melody of the words. The first musical phrase which corresponds to the words *Have you seen?* asks a plaintive question of three notes. Throughout the composition there are similar musical questions. *Before rude hands have touched it?* is treated in much the same way with the phrase ending on a plaintive high,

Have you seen

questioning tone. *Brier* also concludes a question and falls on the highest note in the phrase, a high E. The word *grow* is set to a flight of grace notes ascending from middle E to high G. The lute accompaniment to this flight is a series of rapid chords. Thus while the voice sustains *grow* through a tune of rising scale, the chords are plucked emphatically. The word *fall* drops in a descending flight of notes from high D to middle G. On the word *fire* the voice delays for the space of a half-note while the lute twangs in a rapid series of staccato chords which imply excitement. The exclamatory phrases of the last line are repeated, —the word *sweet* occurring at least three times. The seven " O " and the seven " S " sounds are delayed by half notes, rests and pauses while the lute provides several chords for each word. Naturally the voice lingers over each syllable so that there is ample opportunity for tonal shading.

> Have you seen but a bright lily grow,
> Before rude hands have touch'd it?
> Have you mark'd but the fall of the snow,
>   Before the soil hath smutch'd it?
> Have you felt the wool of the beaver?
>   Or the swan's down ever?
> Or have smelt of the bud of the briar?
>   Or the nard in the fire?
> Or have tasted of the bag of the bee?
> O, so white! O, so soft! O, so sweet is she! [43]

[42] There are two settings for this song differing slightly from each other: Brit. Mus. Add. Mss. 15117; 29481,f.21. For the purposes of this study, the variations in the two MSS. are of very little importance.

[43] Compare " Can you paint a thought? or number? ", *The Broken Heart,* III, 1, John Ford; and " Hast thou seen the down inth' air? " *The Sad One,* IV, 3, Sir John Suckling (song to a lute), and Wm. Cavendish's parody in Act I, Sc. 1, of *The Variety.* These various stanzas apparently inspired more or less by Jonson's song emphasize the popularity of the words with

The fact that Jonson reprinted this song in *Underwoods* shows that he thought it a very good lyric. The third stanza was arranged for music about the year 1615. In 1616 the second and third stanzas appeared together in the play; and all three stanzas were published in the 1640 collection already referred to.

Possibly the tune of the song was an old favorite when Jonson selected it for his third stanza. Wittipol's words to Manly might indicate that the music was well known before the play was produced:

> *Wit.* " Read those:
> (Gives him the copy of the song)
> They'll go unto the air you love so well
> Try them unto the note, may be the music
> Will call her sooner."

Wittipol's explanation may merely be a polite way of introducing the song. But it is possible that Jonson made his lines to suit some popular melody, which was the method of song writing I ventured to think he had employed in the writing of *Drink to me only with thine eyes*.

THE MUSIC FOR THE STAPLE OF NEWS, 1626

The songs in the Staple of News are the last songs in the plays that can be dated. They may be taken to mark the conclusion of Jonson's interest in song for drama. They show, also, a decline in Jonson's power over verbal melody, and over words which suggest tunes. Pennyboy Canter's solo is not strictly narrative nor yet strictly lyrical. The song fails to express a dominating mood, yet it tells no story. The subject matter emphasizes the old miser's love of money, introducing him in a jovial, though

poets and dramatists. Shakespeare's " When daisies pied " (*L. L. L.,* V, 2), though lighter in tone and constructed for quite a different dramatic purpose, has certain qualities in common with Jonson's song, qualities which may suggest why Jonson's song became so popular. Both songs are built up of imagery depicting aspects of nature; both open their best stanza (Jonson's third, and Shakespeare's second) by a reference to flowers; both of these two stanzas are characterized by short easily broken sentences, and many words of pictorial quality, words conveying color ideas, and each contains a sequence of details relating to natural creatures. For an example of great contrast, note Fletcher's serenade in *Monsieur Thomas,* III, 3. Jonson's serenade is an art song, Fletcher's is a popular street song.

ironical vein. The most inviting quality of the song is its rhythm, which smacks of the popular ballad:

> Good morning to my joy! My jolly Pennyboy!
> The lord, and the prince of plenty!
> I come to see what riches, thou bearest in thy breeches,
> The first of thy one and twenty . . . etc.[44]

The other musical skit of the play is a song written by Madrigal. He reads the words first to be sure that no one misses them. Later, Nick, the boy, sings the song to the music of the fiddlers. In harmony with the passion of the hero, the song is a hymn to gold. Pennyboy Junior's appreciation of it emphasizes his joy in the bright product of the mint:

> As bright as is the sun her sire,
> Or earth her mother in her best attire,
> Or Mint, the mid-wife, with her fire,
> Comes forth her grace!
> The splendour of the wealthiest mines
> The stamp and strength of all imperial lines
> Both majesty and beauty shines
> In her sweet face! [45]

Though two stanzas are read aloud, no mention is made of the number of stanzas *sung*. Probably but one received musical setting. The song is rather long, and is interrupted in the reading, so that it does not stand forth in clear cut form.

The Sad Shepherd (Date Unknown)

The last song of importance included in Jonson's plays is the song *Though I am young,* set to music by Nicholas Lanier, printed among Playford's *Select Ayres for Three Voices.*

Jonson's text contains two stanzas of eight lines each. Lanier has used but one in his musical adaptation. Jonson's direction is that Karolin sings "while Aeglamour reads the song." Aeglamour might have read the song while Karolin hummed it; then after the reading, she might have sung it. The theme concerned love and death, always favorite topics with composers: [46]

[44] I, 2.

[45] III, 1. Jonson's two songs about riches are reminiscent of the song beginning, "As light as a fly" from *The Contention between Liberality and Prodigality,*" I, 5.

[46] Thomas May uses the theme in *The Old Couple,* III. Shirley uses it in *Cupid and Death;* and see also *Hamlet,* "In Youth when I did love, did love."

Though I am young and cannot tell
Either what Death or Love is well,
Yet I have heard they both bear darts,
And both do aim at human hearts:
And then again, I have been told,
Love wounds with heat, as Death with cold;
So that I fear they do but bring
Extremes to touch, and mean one thing.[47]

Lanier's setting stresses words such as *young, tell, love, death* and *well,* to emphasize the meaning. *Love wounds with heat* is repeated. The word *darts* falls on a high note, suggesting qualities akin to piercing. The music calls for three parts: Treble, Cantus Secundus, and Bassus.

As a poem, the lyric is praised by anthologists. Jonson himself liked the poem for he indicated that it should be read as well as sung. It was popular as a song in its own time, and was probably sung from the time of its composition for many years following. Playford's selection of it shows that it was among the best of the songs he knew. Its popularity with musicians is probably its best test as a genuine singing lyric. The fact that it may have been arranged as a solo for Karolin and re-arranged as an ayr for three voices by Lanier implies that the song was so closely related to music that it could take several forms of musical notation.

Jonson's career as a playwright presents many vicissitudes of fortune, yet through the twists and turns of fate, it is possible to trace his development as a song writer. There was first of all the feeble song of the cobbler in the *Case is Altered.* Then came a series of songs written for the children, songs expressing the ideals of a young gallant courting a mistress. After Jonson's awakening to the practicality of song in drama, he settled into his career of song writer in business-like fashion, devoting his lyrical efforts to the masques, and reserving but one or two stanzas for his plays. In these plays of the seasoned dramatist we find that each song bears forward the plot, each song serves a definite purpose in identifying character, or in lightening a dull moment. During this period, Jonson created Volpone, who convinced his fair Celia of youthful art and ardor by means of music. Clerimont expressed his restless disposition, and exposed Lady Haughty's secret sins and foibles through melody. Nano painted

[47] I, 2.

his face and made clownish jokes and gestures to draw attention away from the fact that his voice was perhaps unfit for beautiful solo work. Cokes, too, and Nightingale reflected the respective stupidity and cleverness of the Elizabethan gull, and the Elizabethan ballad man.

Like Shakespeare, the more Jonson "gained in experience, the more relevant did he make his songs to their context, and the more important was their office in promoting his dramatic ends." [47] Shakespeare served his apprenticeship in making songs for drama in preparing *A Midsummer Night's Dream,* just as Jonson practiced song-writing in *Cynthia's Revels* and the *Poetaster.* Later in the development of the two playwrights, Balthaser and Volpone, respectively, signify the points in the careers of the dramatists at which an adult singing actor takes a definite part in a play.

But here the parallelism ends; for Shakespeare continued to achieve greater facility in the use of songs in the drama until he reached his crowning glory of mixed plot and lyric in the *Tempest.* Jonson on the other hand, continued to employ songs, but sparingly, in the plays; he developed his dramatic use of music chiefly in connection with the masques. Jonson's masques, however, reveal as subtle a use of song as a dramatist could hope to acquire. His highly specialized control over music for dramatic ends is the study of the next chapter.

Before proceeding with a study of the masques it would be well to sum up the significant evidences of Jonson's lyric ability, from this study of the plays.

The writing of a part song, with its elaborate preparations for repetitions, pictorial treatment, and what-not, demanded concentration upon musical law, and upon the principles governing sixteenth century harmony. The writing of such a song focussed the poet's thoughts upon music. It demanded that he consider all of the possibilities of his lyric for tune and harmony. Naturally the more elaborate the song-form, the greater the necessity for concentrated attention to the laws of music. The more that Jonson wrote songs, the more he needed to think of tunes, to recall the tunes he had already heard, to imagine tunes that might be composed. While subject to the influences of such ideas, he prepared stanzas which were haunted by musical phrases, waver-

[47] For a discussion of *Shakespeare's Use of Song,* see Richmond Noble's book of that title, Oxford Univ. Press, 1923, p. 14, etc.

ing and drooping melodies, gay aires, or mournful refrains.
When his pen formed the letters *Wanton* he must have recalled
other songs which included the word, and remembered how in
each instance the notes wavered and trembled, and the melody
quivered to a little run of grace notes. And remembering this
he knew that he must not extend his line over too many syllables,
but must bring the cadence to an end in order not to extend
the tune through too long a measure. And the more the poet
remembered of music, as he wrote, the more he must have felt
cadences stretching their wings above his lines, until his thoughts,
too, took flight—and fancy and words soared away toward their
destined notes.

Naturally, elaborate songs are more closely akin to music and
make better verbal melody than simple ones. The words which
lend themselves to the difficult intonations of tune and changed
rhythmical beats are easy to read aloud. Almost anyone can speak
Drink to me only with thine eyes and discover verbal melody. But
only with a competent voice can one please oneself or listeners by
singing it. Words which are hard to sing are harder to read, and
words which sing themselves are easy to read. Anyone can read
(in a fashion), but only a chosen few can sing.

The best and most elaborate songs, we have said, make the
best lyric poems for reading. We should have added that the
songs prepared for skilled musicians require an elaborate preparation, which narrative songs like Nano's do not require. Nano's
lines are perhaps more nearly akin to the verses for the printed
page than they are related to music. Jonson did not concentrate
upon musical devices when he made Nano's stanzas. But when
he made Volpone's song he needed to recall how a strong voice
vibrates on full, long vowel sounds, to recall, also which line
lengths, which cadences afford changes of rhythm, and what words
easily bear flights of grace-notes.

We find, then, that the more Jonson concentrated upon music,
the more he prepared for elaborate musical settings, or skilled
singers, the better were his songs, and the more charming were
the stanzas as lyrics. Briefly, let us skim through the plays,
picking out the elaborate songs, and the songs requiring the skill
of an artist, and see if they do not correspond to the lyrics we
would choose if we were anthologists:

From *Cynthia's Revels* and the *Poetaster* we would choose the canzonet, *Slow, slow, fresh fount, Thou more than most, sweet glove, Queen and Huntress, If I freely may discover, She should be allowed her passions, Love is blind, and a wanton, Wake! our mirth begins to die, Then in a Free and lofty Strain*—and we find that these songs have all been commended by the critics. We also note that Jonson was under stress to write songs for the children and that *Cynthia's Revels* and the *Poetaster* contain the largest number of beautiful lyrics in the plays.

From *Volpone* we choose *Come my Celia;* from *Epicœne, Still to be neat,* from *The Devil is an ass, Have you seen but a bright lily grow?* and from the *Sad Shepherd, Though I am young and cannot tell.* These, too, are well known to collectors.

The other songs in the plays were prepared for simple accompaniment, simple tunes to carry forward the plot. They are in fact scraps of plot set to music, narrative in character, and intended for the performance of actors rather than of musicians. Almost any Elizabethan could manage a ballad or a street cry or a narrative song. These songs we should not include in an anthology of lyrics.

In the plays, Jonson was more or less restrained in his use of music; he could not always depend upon a children's company to perform them; he was sometimes forced to import musicians, and to provide for their appearance on the stage. But in the masques he was free to use as many musicians as he chose, and it is in the masques we would expect to find him at the height of his lyric ability, and at the height of his dramatic evaluation of music.

CHAPTER III

THE SONGS IN THE MASQUES

PART I. PROBLEMS OF CONSTRUCTION

Jonson's services as a masque-writer were not confined to scribbling with quill and inkhorn. In many respects his business resembled that of the modern opera director. He shared with the architect, Inigo Jones,[1] the work of designing the stage-settings. He plotted with Giles, Herne, and Lupo over the patterns of the dances.[2] His relations with the musicians were of an even more intimate nature. They could not sing without words, and the order and arrangement of their performance rested entirely on Jonson's calculations. The poet, in turn, depended on the singers to carry out his suggestions in an effective manner. Without their hearty co-operation the masques would never have reached the high state of perfection to which Jonson brought them. Jonson's contacts with some of his co-workers, particularly Inigo Jones, resulted in disastrous quarreling;[3] his relations with the musicians left no record of ill-feeling.

In fact Jonson may have been guided in his planning by the suggestions of the friendly songsters of the court. We know that the poet expressed sincere appreciation for the services of " that most excellent tenor voice and exact singer, her Majesty's servant, Master Jo Allin."[4] Edward Filmer, the Queen's French

---

[1] Jonson mentions his share of designing stage settings in the *Masque of Beauty* (*op. cit.*, p. 51): "Here a curtain was drawn . . . and the scene discovered . . . *which I devised* should be an island floating on a calm water."

[2] In the *Masque of Queens* Jonson praises the motions of the dancers, and follows his words of praise in this fashion: "The author of the dances was Master Thomas Giles," *op. cit.*, p. 128. Mr. Thomas Lupo received £5 for setting the dances to the violins for the Prince's Masque. Pell Records, Issues of the Exchequer for the Reign of James I, May 10, 1611. Herne is commended in the *Masque of Queens*, see *op. cit.*, footnote to page 120.

[3] Herford and Simpson discuss the Jones and Jonson quarrel in the first and second volumes of their *Ben Jonson*. See references in index to Inigo Jones, Vol. II, p. 462.

[4] *Masque of Queens, op. cit.*, p. 128.

composer, also attracted Jonson's admiration.[5] Alphonso Ferrabosco was the subject of a great many tributes from the poet's pen ; [6] and there were hosts of others at his beck and call to whom he might have turned for counsel.

When Jonson blocked out the pattern of a masque, he had at his disposal the most accomplished singers, and the best trained instrumental performers in England. He was at liberty to use as much music as he cared to arrange for—and to prepare his syllables for the tones of exquisite voices or carefully trained polyphonic choruses. He could take into account the size and number of parts in the choruses, as well as the pitch and volume of the soloists' voices.

Before tracing the steps in the production of a masque, we must call to mind the two basic principles of construction: variety and symmetry. Jonson was interested in the problems of symmetry, for he observed the principle in his structures,[7] but he was obsessed by the idea of variety, even for its own sake: he felt that " variety alone was able to refresh and repaire the spirit " [8] and that " we are recreated with change as the stomach is with meats." [9] In addition to these two principles, variety and symmetry, which in a sense govern all forms of artistic endeavor, Jonson was guided by the history and traditions of masque-making.

By the time that Jonson began to write librettos, the court masque had acquired definite form. The favorite amusements of the palace had been joined together and arranged in the pattern of an evening's entertainment, a very elaborate entertainment. In fact, the court masque resembled our modern opera in its fusion of music, spectacle, costume display, and dancing. " The kernel of the show was the masqued dance, in which members of the court, even Queen and King, took part. This dance or masque proper came near the end of the show and was often

[5] Jonson addressed a stanza to Filmer, *Underwoods,* XXVII To Edward Filmer, On His Musical Work, Dedicated to the Queen. " What charming peals are these."

[6] Jonson addressed two *Epigrams* to Ferrabosco, Epigram CXXX and Epigram CXXXI. He praises him also in a footnote to the *Masque of Queens, op cit.,* p. 128.

[7] See Chapter I, pp. 20, 23, 25.

[8] *Discoveries,* ed. G. B. Harrison, E. P. Dutton and Co., New York, p. 71.

[9] *Ibid.*

elaborated into various dances. As accompaniments of this masque were (1) music, instrumental and vocal, (2) a dialogue, taking the form of a play of some length, usually with mythological or allegorical motive, (3) various grotesque dances by professionals, preceding the main masque and often integrated with the play, and (4) a spectacular setting. All of these elements were given great care and expense, and are of interest in various ways." [10] Although Jonson had a share in creating these various elements,[11] his chief responsibility was to write a libretto. Our particular object is the study of the music, both vocal and instrumental, with particular reference to the poet's use of song to further dramatic ends. Before analyzing one of Jonson's musical programs let us consider briefly the importance of music in previous court festivities, and also the significance which masque writers generally attached to the music of the masques.

From the most primitive times, music has accompanied dancing, in fact we cannot imagine successful or pleasurable dancing without music. It is safe to assume that the masque, which was originally a dance, was in its earliest beginnings intimately associated with music.

Perhaps the earliest form of masquing was akin to the simple entertainment Masquerado describes, and ridicules, in *Love Restored*. Masquerado says that there is no musician to play the tunes for the dancers, " nor aught but the wild music " of their own voices, and he knows not what they shall do unless they " come in like a morrice-dance and whistle [their] ballad " themselves.

But the Court Masque, even as early as 1501, has developed far beyond the type of masque that Masquerado suggests. Foreign customs, and new forms of amusement had been added to the original dance, such as processions, gorgeous display of costumes and scenery; moving machinery and mechanical devices had been introduced, and speeches and singing increased the variety and excitement of the entertainment. Each of these new masque elements brought with it a musical accompaniment. During the week of festivities celebrating the marriage of the Prin-

[10] Thorndike, A. H., *Shakespeare's Theater,* New York, The Macmillan Co., 1925, p. 176.
[11] Reyer, Paul, *Les Masques Anglais,* Paris, 1909, p. 427.

cess Katherine of Aragon to Prince Arthur, there were many "pleasant disguisings convayed and shewed in pageants proper and subtile."[12] Two of the disguisings included processions which were accompanied by music.

On Friday evening when all the court was assembled, a wonderfully devised castle was drawn into the hall . . . and "on each of the four turrets sat a little boy . . . who sang sweetly as the pageant advanced down the hall." On the following Thursday there was another maske in "which a pageant moved up the hall towards the King, while two companies of disguisers played so sweetly and with such noyse" that the mirth and merriment "excelled any that was ever enjoyed in England."

The last named pageant was in reality a scenic device as well as a means of bringing in the masquers in procession. The pageant was described as a hill full of all kinds of trees, herbs, and flowers, and on it sat twelve noblemen. Probably the "noyse" which accompanied the progress of the noblemen on their pageant, was intended to drown the screeching of wheels or other sounds of a moving mechanical contraption. Jonson frequently indicated that music was played while gods and goddesses were lowered or raised, or while an island moved forward or backward.

Another significant use of music, and one which Jonson later used to great advantage, was the introduction of important characters to music. When Henry VIII entertained the French ambassadors at Greenwich, "the members of the chapel came in singing, the singers being divided into groups of eight, each group accompanied by a person in rich apparel who engaged in a dialogue or *debat*, 'the effect whereof was whether riches were better than love.'"[13] At the same entertainment another device used by Jonson was apparently employed—that of increasing the importance of the entry of the masquers by playing music as they are introduced. The chronicler devotes some space to describing costumes and the glittering appearance of the masquers, then continues, that, "with minstrelsie these viii noble personages entered."

We see then that early in the history of the English court

[12] There is a full account of this festal occasion included in Enid Welsford's *The Court Masque*, Cambridge, University Press, 1927, pp. 120–121.

[13] Hall's *Chronicles of England, Scotland, and Ireland*, 19th year, quoted and described also by Enid Welsford in *The Court Masque*, p. 144.

masque the various features of the entertainment were accompanied by music. For the purposes of this study it is not necessary to trace the history of the development of music through the various masques presented from the reign of King Henry VIII to that of James I. It would indeed be impossible to trace such a story with any degree of accuracy, for many of the most important writers of masques did not include detailed accounts of the music. Webster and Peele scarcely mention music in their librettos, consequently we know very little about their songs. In fact the amount of music in a masque was more or less dependent upon the fancy of the poet who planned the entertainment. For while Peele and Webster attached little importance to music, Campion made music the outstanding feature of his program. Campion's masques read like descriptions of orchestral effects, enumerations of instruments, enthusiastic accounts of harmonic effects—all interspersed by the words of the songs. Later on, Townsend and Shirley also emphasized the importance of music, but their interest centered in grotesque noises, bird calls, freakish instruments, and motley chatter.

Jonson did not plan for as elaborate musical programs as Campion required, nor did he omit the use of music altogether as did Webster and Peele. His interest centered more in the beauty of melody and harmony than did that of Shirley and Townsend, though he was by no means averse to the use of grotesque music for an anti-masque. Before discussing, however, the "infernal music" of a witches' dance and the imitation of a "Syberaean Quire" in an anti-masque, let us consider the typical program of masque music which Jonson prepared for the court. The musical program for the *Masque of Beauty* furnishes a good example of a Jonsonian musical performance. Careful scrutiny of each of the numbers reveals that music was intimately bound up with the movement, the allegory, the whole being of the masque.

MUSICAL PROGRAM FOR THE MASQUE OF BEAUTY

With settings for the songs arranged by Master Alphonso
Ferrabosco

1. Loud instrumental overture......played by musicians who
were seated in arbours, representing the shades of old poets, and attired like priests in habits of crimson and purple.

2. Full chorus with echoes—" When Love at First Did Move "
......sung by the musicians as
they came forth from their arbours " to the other land," and
" iterated in the closes by two
echoes rising out of the fountains."

3. Tenor solo, " So Beauty on the Waters stood "......" Sung by
a loud tenor."

4. Treble solo, " If all these cupids now were blind "......this
song gave the dancers time to
rest.

5. Treble solo, " It was no policy of court."

6. Tenor solo in answer to the previous treble......" Yes were
the loves or false or straying."

7. Tenor solo, " Had those that dwelt in error foul "......After
galliards and corrantos " the
music appointed to celebrate "
the dancing " could be silent no
longer but admired them thus : "

8. Full chorus, " Still turn and imitate the heavens "......after
the last dance the scene closed
with this full chorus.

The program for the *Masque of Queens* is not a wholly typical
program, nor so elaborate as some of the later entertainments,
but it illustrates the use that Jonson made of harsh, uncouth, discordant music in the anti-masque as a foil for the more dignified,
harmonious, triumphal music accompanying the rest of the entertainment.

THE MUSIC FOR THE MASQUE OF QUEENS

1. " His Majesty, then, being set and the whole company in full
expectation "......Lo u d dis-
cordant instrumental music was
played, and the witches " with a
kind of infernal music came
forth." Their instruments were
all " spindels, timbrels, rattles, or
other venefical instruments, making a confused noise."

2. The witches sing charms while they dance, sometimes describing the instruments they are play-
ing:
   "The dogs they do bay, and the timbrels play,
   And the spindle is now a turning."

3. The last charm includes a change in the character of the music:
   Around, around
   Till a music sound...

   Jonson notes in connection with this musical number that the music was intended to resemble "the Syrbenaean Quires where every man sang what he would without harkening unto his fellow; like the noise of divers oars falling in the water."

   And the pace be found
   To which we may dance
   And our charms advance......

   "At which, with a strange and sudden music, they fell into a magical dance, full of preposterous change and gesticulation. In the heat of their dance on the sudden was heard a sound of loud music, as if many instruments had made one blast"; at this the hags vanished.

4. Loud triumphal music accompanying a change of scene......

   After the disappearance of the hags, a "glorious . . . building figuring the House of Fame" appeared, and music played while Perseus descended from the top of a pyramid.

5. Loud instrumental music plays while the machine turns, and
   as the music ceases, Fame speaks
   . . . etc. . . .

In constructing a masque, the author first blocked out the number of lines to be sung, and the number of lines to be spoken. Usually there were more songs than speeches. The *Masque of Beauty* is composed of eighty lines (omitting the prologue), twenty-four of which are spoken and fifty-six sung. In the *Masque of Hymen* two hundred lines are spoken and (including the polyphonic choruses providing for each phrase to be repeated three times) two hundred and seventy-four lines are sung. The *Hue and Cry* devotes one hundred and sixty-four lines to speeches, and two hundred and ninety-one lines to music.

After making the calculations necessary, Jonson was ready to arrange his material in blocks, dividing the time between speech, song, and dance. There is a great variety of appeal in the arrangement of the *Masque of Beauty,* the structure follows this pattern: speech, *song,* speech, dance, *song,* dance, *song,* speech, *song.* The *Masque of Blackness* followed an equally well balanced arrangement of material, with more symmetrically designed lines of proportion: *song,* dialogue, *song,* dance, *song,* dialogue, dance, *song.* The *Masque of Hymen* is more complicated, but quite as truly proportioned: *song,* speech, *music,* dialogue, *song,* dance, speech, *song,* dance, speech, *song,* dance, speech, *song.* *Love Freed: music,* speech, dance, *song,* speech, *song,* speech, *song,* dance, *song,* revels, dance, *song.*

The next problem was to divide the songs between tenors, trebles and basses. A monotonous series of bass solos was highly undesirable. Or a sequence of high treble voices might destroy an otherwise carefully plotted scheme to gain an effect of variety. Jonson cleverly arranged for a tenor to follow a treble, or a full chorus to come between two bass solos. The *Masque of Beauty* [14] has a very beautiful pattern as far as variety of voices and symmetry of design is concerned; two full choruses balance the beginning and the end of the masque; high pitched voices sing the central songs, and a tenor precedes and follows the treble. This is the order of the design: *full chorus,* tenor, *treble, treble,* tenor, tenor, *full chorus.*

Having outlined the order of treble, tenor and choral songs, Jonson was ready to prepare the words of the stanzas. He knew that he must display each voice to its best advantage, that it would be nothing short of an insult to assign light tripping syl-

[14] *Masque of Beauty, Masques and Entertainments, op. cit.,* pp. 54–57.

lables for the powerful throat of Jo Allin, or the stanzas of a full chorus to a boy's piping treble.

Wherever Jonson marked "tenor solo" on his outline, he knew that he must supplement it with a full sweeping stanza of deep vowel sounds suited to the thundering tones of such a voice as Jo Allin's. The following lines from the *Masque of Beauty* illustrates the use of syllables adapted to the tones of the *loud tenor* who sang them:

> "So Beauty *on* the waters stood
> When Love had severed earth from flood" . . . etc.[15]

In contrast to this song for a loud sweeping tenor, there followed a treble song made up of light, short, staccato syllables, suitable to the modulations of the higher pitch of a boy's or woman's voice: repetitions of dental sounds, and thin short "i's" as well as long "i" sounds prepare for the lighter, higher tones:

> *I*f all these Cup*i*ds now were bl*i*nd
> As *i*s the*i*r wan*t*on brother:
> Or play shoul*d* pu*t* i*t* *i*n their min*d*
> *T*o shoo*t* a*t* one another: . . .[16]

The full song concluding the same masque is written in jarring uneven cadences which would have been highly inappropriate for a soloist. This swellingly robust music required the boisterous volume of a full chorus, and the irregularities of the verbal melody when set to volumes of sound, must have resembled the poetic effect of blank verse. To our ears, unaccustomed to the harmony of a great number of parts, to refrains sustained indefinitely with treble echoes dying and re-dying, sudden clashes of instruments, and loud discordant orchestral sounds blending harmoniously with choral effects, it is difficult to imagine the remarkable ending of a masque. However, the rhythm of the stanza gives us an impression of finality, a sense that all of the odds and ends and wild discordant parts have been drawn into a single chord of unity. The straggling elements have joined in the turning of a large body, into the sweeping exit of a large number of masquers.

---

[15] *Ibid.* The music for this song is in Ferrabosco's *Book of Ayres,* pub. 1609, XXI. (The italics are mine.)

[16] *Op. cit.,* p. 55. Music in Ferrabosco's *Book of Ayres,* XVIII. (The italics are mine.)

> Still turn and imitate the heaven
> In motion swift and even;
> And as his planets go,
> Your brighter lights do so;
> May youth and pleasure ever flow.
> But let your State the while,
> Be fixed as the isle.

Cho.   So that all your beauties sphere,
         May know the Elysian fields are here.
1 Ech.   The Elysian fields are here,
2 Ech.   The Elysian fields are here.[17]

In a general way, then, the problems of masque construction were these: to be on friendly terms with the musicians and performers, to know their abilities, the pitch and volume of their voices; to calculate suitable lines of proportion as to material for singing, and material for the spoken voice; to assign the songs to certain trebles, basses, or tenors; to provide songs made up of syllables which would easily display the artistry of the musicians, and finally, when these problems were presented in outline, the craftsman was ready to turn his attention to the very specific task of making a *beginning*.

PART II—OPENING SONGS

Songs used as a prelude to entertainment of any kind were common enough in the days of Jonson; but he has employed ingenious methods to gain the attention of the audience, to set the mood for the masque, and to introduce characters or situations.

An opening song might have many purposes. After the King with his numerous followers had entered, and the various guests of honor were seated in their places, it was necessary to present something extremely spectacular, something appealing to every possible avenue of the senses, to attract the attention of the audience. Mere pageantry could scarcely compete with the King's own entering parade. A flourish of trumpets would naturally precede the King's entrance. Like the overture to an opera, the first song of the masque quieted the listeners, turned their minds from diplomatic quarrels, or court scandal, and invited concentration on things apart from the ordinary routine of life.

The welcoming song at the beginning of the *Masque of Black-*

[17] *Op. cit.,* p. 57.

ness introduces the main theme. Sung by a triton and two sea maids, " their voices being a tenor and two trebles," and accompanied by " loud music," the song is sufficiently imposing to overcome the noise of late arrivals, and to draw the interest of the audience to the performance. The first words sound the note of welcome, and the remainder of the song states the theme of the masque: that feature, not color, is the proof of beauty. The fullness and roundness of the first line,

> " Sound, sound, aloud,
> The welcome of the orient flood,"

challenges immediate interest and attention. The song gives an impression of loud, swelling, perhaps clashing accompaniment. If, however, the words were arranged to a polyphonic setting, (for instance a canzonet for three voices) the voices could emphasize the first resounding welcome by means of repetitions. The tenor might open the song in this fashion: "*Sound, sound, sound, sound, sound, aloud*" . . . and, while he sustained the third *sound,* the first treble might begin the line; when the tenor came to "*aloud*" the third singer could join the trio. All three would contribute to a swelling crescendo on the tenor's "*aloud.*" The lines of the stanza are of irregular length, the predominance of vowel sounds is well suited to delicate phrasing and subtle intonations. The lyric has appealed to anthologists on account of its verbal melody.

The idea of hospitality (though it relates to the masquers rather than the spectators) is appropriately made the theme of the welcoming strains:

> Sound, sound aloud
> The welcome of the orient flood
> Into the west;
> Fair Niger, son to great Oceanus,
> Now honored thus,
> With all his beauteous race:
> Who, though but black in face,
> Yet are they bright,
> And full of life and light,
> To prove that beauty best
> Which not the color but the feature
> Assures unto the creature.[19]

[19] *Masque of Blackness,* p. 38.

A procession, pouring forth from two sides of the stage, opens the *Masque of Hymen*. First came five pages " attired in white, bearing five tapers of virgin wax "—On the other hand entered Hymen . . . in a saffron colored robe. After him a youth attired in white bearing another light, behind him two others in white bearing distaff and spindle, . . . betwixt these a personated bride. In the midst went the Auspices, after them two that sung in several coloured silks. Of which one bore the water, the other the fire; last of all the musicians diversely attired, all crowned with roses "; and " with this SONG began:

> Bid all profane away; [20]
> None here may stay
> To view our mysteries,
> But who themselves have been,
> Or will in time be seen,
> The self-same sacrifice.
> For Union, mistress of these rites,
> Will be observed with eyes
> As simple as her nights.

Cho.:
> Fly then all profane away,
> Fly far off as hath the day;
> Night her curtain doth display,
> And this is Hymen's holy-day. [21]

The function of this song was to put the audience in an expectant humour. The words imply that something interesting and important will follow and those who are out of sympathy with the theme are invited to leave at once. The outline of the masque and the mood of suspense are introduced simultaneously. Holiness, supernatural elements, and pomp are implied in the words *profane, mysteries, display.* The mood is set, and " The song being ended, Hymen presented himself," his appearance heralded by the introduction of his name in the last line:

" And this is Hymen's holy-day."

The dialogue preceding the actual opening of the masque, *Love Restored,* suggests that the only proper way to begin a masque is by means of music. " The King and Court being seated, and

[20] Shirley's *Triumph of Peace* begins the masque proper with similar lines: Irene sings: Hence, ye profane, far hence away!
            Time hath sick feathers while ye stay.
[21] *Op. cit.,* p. 60.

in expectation," a certain Masquerado came forth, announcing
there could be no masque for there was not a musician present,
and the masquers would have to do with wild music; the play boy
which acted Cupid was so hoarse he could not be heard. "Unless we should come in like a morris-dance, and whistle our
ballad ourselves, I know not what we should do: we have neither
musician to play our tunes." [22]

The masque finally opens with the entrance of Cupid in his
chariot, guarded by masquers, in number ten, singing this song:

> O how came Love, that is himself a fire,
>   To be so cold?
> Yes, tyrant Money quencheth all desire,
>   Or makes it old.
> But here are beauties will revive
> Love's youth, and keep his heat alive:
>   As often as his torch here dies,
>   He need but light it at fresh eyes.
> Joy, joy the more: for in all courts,
> If Love be cold so are his sports.[23]

The song plunges the audience into the middle of the action.
It explains the situation, with all that has preceded the entrance
of Cupid. The God of Love has been out of humour, due to
the influence of the tyrant, Money. The purpose of the masquers
is to restore his native good spirits. The entrance of the real
Cupid is strikingly contrasted with the impostor Cupid, who
merely walked on the stage according to the instruction " Enter,
Plutus, as Cupid." [24]   The personal qualities of the chief character
are gracefully praised at the time of his entrance, emphasizing
his passionate nature, his aptitude for joy, and the idea that he
was a sort of spoiled-small-boy-god.

Mercury Vindicated opened to "Loud music. After which
the Scene is discovered; being a Laboratory or Alchemist's work-
house: Vulcan looking to the registers, while a Cyclope, tending
the fire, to the cornets began to sing:

Cyc.: Soft, subtile fire, thou soul of art,
        Now do thy part
    On weaker nature, that through age is lamed.
        Take but thy time, now she is old,

[22] *Love Restored, op. cit.,* p. 166.
[23] *Ibid.,* p. 171.
[24] *Love Restored, op. cit.,* p. 166.

> And the sun her friend grown cold,
> She will no more in strife with thee be named.
>
> Look, but how few confess her now,
>   In cheek or brow!
> From every head, almost, how she is frighted!
>   The very age abhors her so,
>   That it learns to speak and go,
> As if by art alone it could be righted." [25]

The loud music preceding the song commanded the attention of the audience. Contrasting with the triumphant, or perhaps, imposing " loud music," the " soft music" naturally caused each listener to strain his ears to catch the significance of what followed. Soft music following loud music is always very effective in gaining the attention of an audience.

The Cyclop's song presents many of the artifices of the song-writer. There are irregular line lengths, symmetrical stanzas of identical metrical pattern and syllables suited to vocalising. The words *soft, fire, weaker, lamed* and *strife* might appeal to a composer for pictorial treatment. Editors have presented the stanza for its lyric beauty in collections of Elizabethan verse.

The soft accompaniment of cornet music was very subtly chosen to increase the dramatic significance of the situation. The timbre of the cornet is akin to that of the trumpet, with a faint association of war, fire, and sudden sacking of cities. Even though music is performed softly, the tones of the cornet contribute subtle suggestions of a mysterious terror in the cave's gloomy depths. There is parallelism in the stirring opening music, followed by softened sweet strains—and the ruder elements of the beginning of the masque followed by the more elaborate and beautiful spectacle which succeeded. The loud music might also suggest that a fire had but just been roaring in the cave; while the soft music indicates that the Cyclop has gained control over the raging of the element, and that vindication is approaching. The theme of the masque is set forth clearly: a contest between art and nature. The words " as if " imply that art *alone* can never succeed.

Pleasure Reconciled to Virtue opens to a " wild music of cymbals, flutes and tabors " accompanying the entrance of the god Comus who issued from a grove of ivy riding in triumph, crowned

---

[25] *Mercury Vindicated, op. cit.,* p. 187.

with roses and attended by followers who join in the full chorus beginning:

"Room! room! make room for the Bouncing Belly," [26]

The clashing of cymbals, shrill abandon of lutes, with the noise of a tabor might well symbolize the character of the god Comus. Cymbals had been used since Biblical times to herald festivity, religious dance or the triumph of a conquering army. In England, says Cowling, "the tabor was commonly used for accompanying morris dances at rural merry-makings." [27] The entire hymn must have proceeded in rude barbaric manner. Jonson describes the effect in this way: "every man stands under the eaves of his own hat and sings what pleases him." [28]

The words, "Room, room," challenge the on-lookers, suggesting the approach of an important personage, and one of considerable size. The song embodies the spirit of the first part of the masque, a spirit of vulgar, jarring, crude, but wild good humor and gross wit.

Contrasting vividly with the opening of *Pleasure Reconciled*, *Chloridia* presents a pleasant scene, and a serene sky with transparent clouds: "in a part of the air, a bright cloud begins to break forth; and in it is sitting a plump boy, in a changeable garment, richly adorned, representing the mild Zephyrus." [29]

The boy begins to sing "Come forth, come forth," a song to lure the spring; and Spring replies from a purple cloud, "It is already done." The dialogue song gives the key to the situation, the mood and spirit of the masque. The stanzas have been sought out by collectors of anthologies. The poet arranged his lines cleverly to appeal to the composer's art. The first line has the same kind of inviting beginning as the *Come away* songs discussed in Chapter II, page 51. The underscored words are suitable for pictorial treatment, while the last line of the chorus rises to a peculiarly triumphant ring. The questions and answers afford dramatically rising and falling cadences, and the alterations of dialogue with homophonic and polyphonic measures must have been extremely intriguing to the musicians.

[26] *Pleasure Reconciled*, p. 222.
[27] Cowling, G. H., *Music on the Shakespearean Stage*, Cambridge Univ. Press, 1913, p. 58.
[28] *Pleasure Reconciled, op. cit.*, p. 223.
[29] *Chloridia, op. cit.*, p. 368.

While "Come forth" is a bit challenging, and draws the attention of the audience, the gentle words which follow present an idyllic atmosphere, soft, yielding, and graceful in its lyrical expression.

First Song

Zeph.:   Come forth, come forth, the gentle Spring,
       And carry the glad news I bring
          To earth, our common Mother;
       It is decreed by all the gods
       That heaven of earth shall have no odds,
       But one shall love another.

       Their glories they shall mutual make,
       Earth look on heaven for heaven's sake,
          Their honours shall be even:
       All emulation cease, and jars,
       Jove will have earth to have her stars
          And lights, no less than heaven.

Spring: It is already done, in flowers
       As fresh and new as are the hours,
          By warmth of yonder sun:
       But will be multiplied on us,
       If from the breath of Zephyrus
          Like favor we have won.

Zeph.:   Give all to him; his is the dew,
       The heat, the humour,
Spring: —All the true
       Beloved of the spring!
Zeph.:   The sun, the wind, the verdure!
Spring: —All
       That wisest Nature cause can call
       Of quickening anything." [30]

Frequently there was instrumental music preceding a masque. It is more difficult to judge the function of the songs without words, yet Jonson's descriptions contain clues as to the character of the tunes. Generally speaking the instrumental overtures were used for the same purposes as the verses set to music.

Jonson hints at the nature of the instrumental music which preceded *Love Freed:* "So soon as the King's Majesty was set, and in expectation, there was heard a strange music of wild instruments. To which a Sphynx came forth dancing, leading Love bound." [31]

[30] *Chloridia,* pp. 368, 369.
[31] *Love Freed,* p. 156.

The strange music of wild instruments was appropriate for the introduction of a barbaric sphynx. It added, no doubt, a certain mysterious horror to his villainy. The effect of the music was apparently discordant, crude, compared with the harmonious songs celebrating the freedom of Love. The instruments thus designated by Jonson as *wild,* were tied up with twenty-four yards of ribbon; [32] and the strange noise resulted very likely from a combination of hoboyes, violins, sackbuts, lutes and flutes.[33]

The *Golden Age Restored* opens to "loud music": "Pallas and her chariot descending, to a softer music." The loud music announced the beginning of the masque, demanding order in the audience, while the soft music set the mood for the reception of a gentle feminine deity. The entrance of Pallas is reminiscent of the Mystery Plays in which soft music lent an atmosphere of awe or enchantment to the presence of God and the Angels.

PART III.   MUSIC IN THE MAIN BODY OF A MASQUE

Songs served such a variety of purposes throughout the main body of a masque that it is difficult to classify them. The appearance or discovery of the masquers, generally held to be the climax of a masque, was emphasized by music. Sometimes the masquers came in singing, explaining their actions, or interpreting situations. Single characters soliloquized in song. Persuasive songs invited nymphs to dance, or water fairies to come forth from the sea. Occasionally songs took the place of dialogue. Scenic effects were appropriately emphasized through accompanying songs, and the noises involved in squeaking machinery suitably overwhelmed by strains of music.[35]   Brazen compliments

[32] Pell Records, see footnote 2, on page 78 of this chapter.

[33] *Ibid.*

[35] Other writers indicate that descents and moving about on the stage, especially motion involving machinery was accompanied by music. Samuel Daniel notes in the *Vision of the Twelve Goddesses,* that "The Graces march before the Goddesses, descending . . . with loud music." *English Masques, op. cit.,* p. 14. Campion's description in the *Lord's Masque* is to the same effect: "According to the humour of this song, the stars moved in an exceeding strange and delightful manner, and I suppose few have ever seen more neat artifice than Master Inigo Jones shewed in contriving their motion." *Eng. Masques, ibid.,* p. 78. Again Campion notes: "on this cloud the masquers, led by Prometheus, descended with the music of a

addressed to the King took on an air of subtlety and grace when
set to musical accompaniment.

The *Masque of Lethe* prepares cleverly for the appearance of
the masquers. Those who danced the Antimasque retired into
the grove, "before the last person be off the stage, the first Couple
appear in their posture between the trees, ready to come forth,
changed."[36] The short intervening dialogue and chorus give
the remainder of the dancers time to complete the change. The
song itself is essential to the sense of the story:

Cho.:   "Return, return,
          Like lights to burn,
                  On earth
                  For others good:
          Your second birth
          Will fame old Lethe's flood;
                  And warn a world,
                  That now are hurled
          About in tempest, how they prove
                  Shadows for Love.
          Leap forth: your light it is the nobler made,
          By being struck out of a shade."

The words "leap forth" give the signal for the masquers to
return, and after the conclusion of the last line "they dance forth
their entry, or first dance." The content of the song is very
nearly a resumé of the theme of the masque. The last two lines
emphasize the lighting arrangement, the effect of the appearance
of the masquers coming forth from a dark wood into the full
light of the stage. The purpose of the return of the masquers
is stated, and the statement that the change has been a re-birth in
spirit as well as in form, marks the turning point of the masque.

The discovery of the masquers in *Time Vindicated* requires a
great deal of musical assistance. After the second antimasque,
there is,

> "Loud music.

To which the whole Scene opens; where Saturn sitting with
Venus is discovered above, and certain votaries coming forth below, which are the chorus." After a speech from Fame, clos-

full song." *Ibid.*, p. 79. Davenant in his *Salmacida Spolia* describes
two celestial persons in a silver chariot breaking through a cloud, and
"these in their descent sung together." *Ibid.*, p. 233.

[36] *Masque of Lethe*, p. 212.

ing " Expect," there is a musical dialogue between Venus and Saturn at the close of which the " Masquers are discovered and that which obscured them vanisheth."

Jonson's description of the discovery of the masquers in *Neptune's Triumph* is of interest. The moving of the island may have caused rumbling or squeaking of mechanical devices. The song following the discovery is a direct compliment to the Prince. The effect of high climax, or intense interest is sustained through the songs that follow until the " island goes back . . . the upper Chorus takes it from them, and the MASQUERS prepare for their figure." The first discovery of the masquers occurred after the antimasque :

" *Poet:* ' Well now, expect the scene itself : it opens! ' "

The island of Delos is discovered, the Masquers sitting in their several sieges.   The heavens opening, and Apollo, with Mercury, some of the Muses, and the Goddess Harmony, make the music : the while the island moves forward, Proteus sitting below, and Apollo sings :

Song

Apol.:   Look forth, the shepherd of the seas,
And of the ports that keep'st the keys,
   And to your Neptune tell,
His Albion, prince of all his isles,
For whom the sea and land so smiles,
   Is home returned well.

Grand Cho.: And be it thought no common cause
That to it so much wonder draws,
   And all the heavens consent
With Harmony to tune their notes
In answer to the public votes
   That for it up were sent.
It was no envious step dame's rage,
Or tyrant's malice of the age,
   That did employ him forth;
But such a wisdom that would prove
By sending him their hearts and love
   That else might fear his worth.

By this time the island hath joined itself with the shore; and Proteus, Portunus, and Saron come forth, and go up singing to the State, while the MASQUERS take time to land."

Songs persuading dancers to dance or not to dance, to come or to go, take the place of words in forwarding the action. The *Masque of Blackness* illustrates the use of a provocative song: . . . " as they were about to make choice of their men: one, from the sea, was heard to call them with this charm, sung by a tenor voice." Ferrabosco wrote the music for this song, and included it in his *Book of Ayres*. The tenor is accompanied by the lute.

> Come away, come away,
> We grow jealous of your stay ;
> If you do not stop your ear,
> We shall have more cause to fear
> Syrens of the land than they
> To doubt the Syrens of the sea.

" Here they danced with their men several measures and corantos. All which ended, they were again accited to sea, with a song of two trebles, whose cadences were iterated by a double echo from several parts of the land." [38]

In the *Masque of Hymen,* Jonson again employed song to introduce dancing:

" By this time the ladies were paired with the men, and the whole sixteen ranked forth, in order, to dance: and were with this SONG provoked.

> Now, now, begin to set
> Your spirits in active heat ;
> And since your hands are met,
> Instruct your nimble feet,
> In motions swift and meet,
> The happy ground do beat ;

Cho.:
> Whilst all this roof doth ring,
> And each discording string,
> With every varied voice,
> In union doth rejoice.

Here they danced forth a most neat and curious measure, full of subtlety and device, which was so excellently performed, as it

---

[38] *Blackness,* p. 43. The popularity of *Come away* songs has been commented on in Chapter II, p. 51. The *Come away* song was useful to further action within the masque as well as for an exit song. Campion used it in the *Lord's Masque:*

> Come away; bring thy golden theft,
> . . . .
> Come quickly, come! . . .

seemed to take away that spirit from the invention, which the invention gave to it: and left it doubtful whether the forms flowed more perfectly from the author's brain, or their feet." [39]

A little later in the same masque another song provoked the dancers: " The speech being ended, they dissolved: and all took forth other persons (men and women) to dance other measures, galliards, and corantos: the whilst this SONG importuned them to a fit remembrance of the time.

> Think yet, how night doth waste,
> How much of time is past,
> What more than winged haste
> Yourselves would take,
> If you were but to taste
> The joy the night doth cast
> (O might it ever last)
> On this bright virgin and her happy make.

Their dances yet lasting," etc. . . .[40]

In fact the *Masque of Hymen* is largely a series of songs and dances, the songs being used to introduce the dances. In the *Masque of Oberon* the masquers were excited to dance by a song, and invited home,—thus clearing the stage, and preparing for the final closing of the machine.[41] The words of the songs were made to connect the dances, thus serving as a unifying element drawing both song and dance toward a single purpose.

Usually the songs filled a number of offices. They were primarily required, as any song might be, to entertain because of their own aesthetic beauty. In *Hymen* it is desirable for the priests to offer an invocation at the altar of Juno. The invocation is presented as a song, which is not only a feature of interest in itself, but represents ritual, and sets a mystic atmosphere for the descent of Juno. " Their descent was made in two great clouds, that put forth themselves severally, and, with one measure of time, were seen to stoop, and fall gently down upon the earth . . . Whilst they were descending this song was sung at the altar.[42]

> These, these are they,
> Whom Humour and Affection must obey;
> Who come to deck the genial bower

[39] *Hymen,* p. 69.
[40] *Hymen,* p. 70.
[41] *Masque of Oberon,* p. 154.
[42] *Hymen,* p. 67.

And bring with them the grateful Hour
That crowns such meetings, and excites
The married pair to fresh delights;
As courtings, kissings, coyings, oaths and vows,
Soft whisperings, embracements, all the joys
And melting toys,
That chaster love allows.

Chorus:

Haste, haste, for Hesperus his head down bows." [43]

In the *Masque of Oberon,* the Satyrs quarrel as to whether they shall spend their time in brawling, or in making music. They decide to sing, and entertain themselves as well as the audience. The song begins,

" Now, my cunning lady: moon," [44]

appropriately emphasizing the setting which was " all obscure, and nothing perceived but a dark rock, with trees beyond it, and all wildness that could be presented: till, at one corner of the cliff, above the horison, the moon began to show, and rising, a Satyr was seen by her light." [45]

In *Love Freed* the Muse's Priests advance to the rescue of Love singing a song to interpret their purpose. The song is a brazen explanation of the situation, essential to the movement of the plot:

Gentle love, be not dismayed.
See the Muses pure and holy,
By their priests have sent thee aid
Against this brood of Folly.
It is true, that Sphynx their dame
Had the sense first from the Muses
Which in uttering she doth lame,
Perplexeth and abuses.
But they bid that thou shouldst look
In the brightest face here shining,
And the same, as would a book,
Shall help thee in divining." [46]

[43] Fletcher uses an altar-scene, with a song of invocation in the *Mad Lover:* Scene, the Temple of Venus . . . enter Clais, Lucippe, Cleanthe, and her train with lights, singing:

Oh, fair sweet goddess, queen of loves,
Soft and gentle as thy doves, . . . etc.

[44] *Oberon,* p. 150.
[45] *Oberon,* p. 143.
[46] *Love Freed,* p. 163.

82615

The bard's song in the *Irish Masque* draws together the various possible meanings of the preceding action and summarizes the various meanings in the masque. The whole is presented as a compliment to the King.[47]   The introduction of the bard is carefully prepared for:

Gent.: Advance immortal Bard, come up and view
The gladding face of that great king, in whom
So many prophecies of thine are knit.
. . . .
Sing them some charm, made from his present looks,

Here the Bard sings to two harps.

Song

Bow both your heads at once and hearts;
Obedience doth not well in parts.
It is but standing in his eye,
You'll feel yourselves changed by and by.
Few live, that know, how quick a spring
Works in the presence of a king:
'Tis done by this; your slough let fall,
And come forth new-born creatures all.

During this song, the Masquers let fall their mantles, and discover their masquing apparel. Then they dance forth.[48]

One excuse for inserting a song was to awaken sleepers. In the *Golden Age Restored,* Pallas bids the spirits sing to awaken certain blessed souls sleeping in Elysian bowers:

Pal.: Then see you yonder souls, set far within the shade,
That in Elysian bowers the blessed seats do keep,
That for their living good, now semi-gods, are made,
And went away from earth as if but tamed with sleep;
These we must join to wake . . ."[49]

The chorus responds to Pallas' direction:

[47] Shirley presented compliments to royalty in the form of songs: " Then the whole train of musicians move in a comely figure toward the King and Queen, and bowing to the state, this following ode is sung:" Shirley, James, *Triumph of Peace, ibid.,* p. 221.   In the same masque the Hours and Chori again move toward the state and sing: " live Royal Pair," etc., pp. 223, 224. Davenant also presents his Song to the Queen Mother in a similar fashion: " they [chorus] go up to the State and sing." *Salmacia Spolia, op. cit.,* p. 238.

[48] *Irish Masque,* pp. 185–186.

[49] *Golden Age,* p. 197.

Cho.: " Awake, awake, for whom these times were kept,[50]
O wake, wake, wake, as you had never slept!
Make haste and put on air, to be their guard
Whom once but to defend is still reward."

Pleasure Reconciled to Virtue employs another song to arouse a sleeper. The Pygmies danced for joy: " At the end of their Dance they thought to surprise " the sleeping Hercules who was " suddenly . . . awaked by the music. He roused himself, and they all ran into holes. The stanza is exceedingly suggestive of dramatic chords, pauses, and pictorial treatment.

Song

Wake, Hercules, awake; but heave up thy black eye,
'Tis only asked from thee to look, and these will die,
Or fly—
Already they are fled,
Whom scorn has else left dead." [51]

Pleasure Reconciled is divided into portions separated from each other by antimasques. Two of the sections are carefully joined together, so that the parts appear to belong to a single unified whole. Jonson used a song as the connecting link between these two parts. Hercules entered and spoke at length bidding the Grove to vanish. At the conclusion of his words, " the Grove and Antimasque vanished, and the whole Music was discovered. sitting at the foot of the mountain, with Pleasure and Virtue seated above them." [52]

The chorus then addresses Hercules asking him to sleep, and suggesting that Virtue weave a crown for him, while he sleeps.

[50] *Ibid.,* p. 198. Compare with the song Shakespeare uses to waken Gonzalo : (Sings in Gonzalo's ear :)

> While you here do snoring lie,
> Open-eyed Conspiracy . . . etc.
> Awake, Awake!—*Tempest,* Act I, Sc. 1.

Dekker's Priest of the Sun (Dramatic Works of Thomas Dekker, London, 1873, 4 volumes) awakens sleeping Raybright at the beginning of the play with an *Awake* song. The song begins slowly, and dreamily, as if the priest is in no hurry to arouse the sleeper. The last two lines were probably sung with more spirit, and a bit louder, than the rest:

> Thoughts Flie away, Time hath past 'em;
> Wake now, awake, see and taste 'em.
>   *The Sun's Darling,* Act I, Sc. 1.

[51] *Pleasure Reconciled,* p. 226.
[52] Pleasure Reconciled, p. 225.

Hercules lies down and slumbers while the chorus sings a song, at the close of which another anti-masque enters. Thus the song fills in the time between the two antimasques, supplying a logical step in the progress of the action:

Song

Cho.:　　Great friend and servant of the good,
　　　　　Let cool awhile thy heated blood
　　　　　And from thy mighty labour cease,
　　　　　Lie down, lie down,
　　　　　And give thy troubled spirits peace:
　　　　　Whilst Virtue, for whose sake
　　　　　Thou dost this godlike travail take,
　　　　　May of the choicest herbage make,
　　　　　Here on this mountain bred,
　　　　　A crown, a crown
　　　　　For thy immortal head." [53]

Parts of *Pleasure Reconciled* are so intertwined with music and speeches, and action, that it is impossible to separate the three elements without seriously damaging the sense of the performance. The songs contain directions for the movement of the actors, they explain what is happening, they prepare for what is to happen.

" Here the whole choir of music called the twelve MASQUERS forth from the top of the mountain, which then opened, with this

[53] *Ibid.* Fletcher's song in honour of Virtue was used for a ceremonial rite. Mountferrat is led to the altar and divested of his office, later Miranda is led to the altar and invested with new office, and takes new vows. First song:
　　　　　See, see the stain of honour, Virtue's foe,
　　　　　Of virgin's fair fames the foul overthrow! etc. . . .
Second song:
　　　　　Fair child of Virtue, Honour's bloom,
　　　　　That here with burning zeal dost come . . . etc.
　　　　　　　　　—*The Knight of Malta,* Act B, V, Sc. 2.
In *Old Fortunatus* Dekker uses two songs in honour of Virtue. The first song is a wail of a priest decrying the neglect of the goddess. The second is a song of praise and rejoicing that Virtue has received her proper homage:
Priest:　　Virtue's branches wither, virtue pines,
　　　　　Pittie, Pittie and alacke the time, etc.
The *Rejoicing* song closes Dekker's play:
　　　　　Virtue smiles, crie hollyday, etc.
　　　　　. . . . .
　　　　　Sing hymnes to Virtue's deity,
　　　　　Sing hymnes to Virtue's deity.

Song

Ope, aged Atlas, open then thy lap,
And from thy beamy bosom strike a light,
That men may read in the mysterious map
    All lines,
    And signs
Of royal education, and the right,
See how they come and show,
That are but born to know.
    Descend,[54]
    Descend;
Though pleasure lead,
Fear not to follow:
They who are bred
Within the hill
    Of skill,
May safely tread
What path they will
No ground of good is hollow.[55]

" In their descent from the hill, Daedalus came down before them," then followed a short dialogue between Daedalus and Mercury, at the close of which the dancers, " put themselves in form," and " Daedalus had his first song; " the song describes the dance which followed, and bids the dancers begin:

Come on, come on, and where you go,
So interweave the curious knot,
As even the observer scarce may know
Which lines are Pleasure's and which not," [57]

[54] See Shirley's use of the *Descend* device in *Triumphs of Peace,* quoted on page 23. Townsend employed many of Jonson's devices. His chariot ascends to music, and while the masquers are descending one sings " come down "—*Ablion's Triumph.*

Middleton's Masque of the Inner Temple contains short lines breaking the longer body of the song, to which a descent is made:

    I am down
    To crown

His *Triumph of Truth* contains a rising song:

    Thy aged eyes, To see him rise, etc.

[55] *Pleasure Reconciled,* p. 229.

[57] The *Triumph of Beauty* celebrates graces and invites the masquers to dance or revel in a dialogue song: (Sung by Hymen and Delight).

Hymen.:   Come, ye Graces, come away;
Delight: Ye pleasant Hours, why do you stay?
                —Shirley, *Triumph of Beauty.*
Campion prepared an interesting dancing song for his Entertainment for

The continuing verses must certainly have been written in collaboration with the dancing master who designed the figures:

First figure out the doubtful way,
At which a while all youth should stay,
Where she and Virtue did contend
Which should have Hercules to friend.

Then as all actions of mankind
Are but a labyrinth or maze:
So let your dances be entwined,
Yet not perplex men unto gaze,

But measured, and so numerous too,
As men may read each act they do;
And when they see the graces meet,
Admire the wisdom of your feet.

For dancing is an exercise,
Not only shows the mover's wit
But maketh the beholder wise,
As he hath power to rise to it.

HERE THE FIRST DANCE

In *News from the New World* the singing and dancing unite

Lord Knowles: . . . " they present a song with five parts, and withal a lively sylvan dance of six persons: the Robin-hood men feign two trebles; one of the Keepers with the Cynic sing two counter tenors, the other Keeper, the bass, but the Traveller being not able to sing, gapes in silence, and expresseth his humour in antic gestures: "

Dance now and sing; the joy and love we owe
Let cheerful gestures and glad gestures show:
(Voices)
The Queen of grace as she whom we receive . . . etc., *op. cit.,* p. 179.

The *Lord's Masque* also contains a dancing song:

Advance your choral motions now,
Your music-loving lights: . . . etc. . . .
Once more again, yet nearer move
Your forms at willing view; . . . etc., *op. cit.,* p. 198.

According to the humour of this song, " the stars moved in an exceeding strange and delightful manner," etc.   The same masque contains another dancing song beginning " Dance, dance! and visit now the shadows of our joy," etc.   The second verse continues the idea of motion: " Turn, turn! and honour now the life these figures bear," *op. cit.,* p. 207. Middleton's *Masque of the Inner Temple* contains a dancing song similar in motive " Move on, move on, be still the same," pp. 214–15. Daniel's *Masque of the Twelve Goddesses* contains a dance-song, sung by the Graces, beginning,

Whiles worth with honor make their choice
For measured motions ordered right.

. . . In *Tethy's Festival,* Tethys sings: " If joy had other figure," etc. (while the others dance).

in carrying on the main idea or plot of the masque. The songs emphasize the scenic effects, draw attention to the icicle costumes, praise the dancing and add whatever philosophical significance there is to the procedure. The Fourth Song is a soliloquy by Fame, explaining her purpose in singing. Apart from the words of the songs there is very little thought-content in the latter part of the masque.

" Here the Scene opens, and discovers the Region of the Moon, from which the MASQUERS descend, and shake off their icicles.

First Song

Howe'er the brightness may amaze,
Move you, and stand not still at gaze,
As dazzled with the light:
But with your motions fill the place,
And let their fullness win you grace,
Till you collect your sight.
So while the warmth you do confess
And temper of these rays no less
To quicken than refine,
You may by knowledge grow more bold,
And so more able to behold
The body whence they shine.
          THE FIRST DANCE FOLLOWS

Second Song

Now look and see in yonder throne," [58]

The remainder of the song praises the King, and introduces the main dance and revels. The third song immediately follows the revels, telling the Masquers that the King is responsible for joy on earth, and bidding them speak about the world from whence they came. The last dance is followed by the FOURTH SONG:

" Look, look already where I am,
     Bright Fame,
Got up unto the sky,
     Thus high,
Upon my better wing,
     To sing
The knowing king,
And made the music here,
With yours on earth the same."

[58] *News from the New World*, pp. 250, 251, 252.

Chorus:　Join then to tell his name,
　　　　　And say but James is he;
　　　　　All ears will take the voice
　　　　　And in the tune rejoice,
　　　　　Or Truth hath left to breathe, and Fame hath left to
　　　　　　be." [59]

In the description of *Love's Triumph,* Jonson mentions "an applausive SONG, or pæan of the whole; which she [fame] takes occasion to ingeminate in the SECOND CHORUS, upon the sight of a work of Neptune's, being a hollow rock, filling part of the sea prospect, whereon the muses sit."

Hymn

Euc.:　So Love emergent out of Chaos brought
　　　　　The world to light!
　　　　And gently moving on the waters, wrought
　　　　All form to sight!
　　　　Love's appetite
　　　　Did beauty first excite:
　　　　And left imprinted in the air
　　　　Those signatures of good and fair,

Cho.:　Which since have flowed, flowed forth upon the sense
　　　　To wonder first and then to excellence! [60]
　　　　By virtue of divine intelligence!

Jonson depended upon harmonic effects to emphasize qualities of character. The introduction of Comus to a wild music of strange instruments has been previously discussed.[61]

[59] *Ibid.,* p. 252.

[60] *Love's Triumph,* pp. 364–365.

[61] See page 92 of this chapter. Campion describes accompaniments definitely intended to emphasize character: "till by virtue of a new change in the music, the Lunatics fell into a mad measure, fitted to a loud fantastic tune; but in the end thereof the music changed into a very solemn air, which they softly played, while Orpheus spake."—*Lord's Masque,* English Masques, *op. cit.,* p. 74. Beaumont indicates similar devices in his *Masque of the Inner Temple:* "at their coming" [the Statuas] "the air of the music was utterly turned into a soft time, with drawing notes, excellently expressing their natures, and the measure likewise fitted unto the same." The effect resulted from the music changing "from violins to hautboys, cornets, etc." *Ibid.,* p. 94. Beaumont remarks further in the same masque on the accompaniment of the anti-masque: "the music was extremely well fitted, having such a spirit of country jollity as can hardly be imagined." *Ibid.,* p. 95.

Shirley describes certain musical effects in his *Triumph of Peace,* emphasizing character: "Here variety of other antick music, counterfeiting the voices of birds; and after these (in a procession) rode a Magpie, a Crow, a Jay, and a Kite in a quadrangular figure and in the midst an Owl." *Ibid.,* p. 206.

In the *Golden Age Restored,* the nature of the *Evils* is strikingly emphasized by the type of music which accompanies their dance. " The Evils enter for the Antimasque and Dance, to two drums, trumpets, and a confusion of martial music." [62] In contrast to this type of music Pallas had already descended to soft music.[63]   And after the Antimasque Pallas commands that the kind of music be changed, so that the accompaniment will be more suitable for the descent of Astrea and the Golden Age:

> Descend, you long, long wished and wanted pair,
> And as your softer times divide the air,
> So shake all clouds off with your golden hair . . ." [64]

The song of the two women in the *Masque for the Honour of Wales,* is a rough, coarse song, intended to emphasize the crude and primitive state of the provincial Welsh.   The women take turns in singing line about, which would add to the choppy effect of the dialectic chatter.

Song

1. Wom.:   Au, God bless it our good king Sames,
            His wife and his sildren, and aull his reams,
2. Wom.:   And aull his ursipful sistice of peace about him,
1. Wom.:   And send that his court be never without him.
2. Wom.:   Ow, that her would come down into Wales,
1. Wom.:   Her sud be very welcome to Welse Ales.
2. Wom.:   I have a cow,
1. Wom.:   And I have a hen;
2. Wom.:   Sall give it milk,
1. Wom.:   And eggs for aull his men.
Both: Itself sall have benison and other seere,
            And may it be starved that steal him his deer,
            There, there, and everywhere.[65]

Venus praises her own qualities in a song-soliloquy, declaring her power, her ability, drawing attention to her appearance, the girdle she wears, and her raison d'être.   A less subtile description in the first person could scarcely be presented on the stage,[66] yet the brazen effect is softened when the words are sung.

---

[62] *The Golden Age Restored,* p. 196.
[63] *Ibid.,* p. 196.   [64] *Ibid.,* p. 196.
[65] *For the Honour of Wales,* p. 240.
[66] Fletcher's Orpheus comes from Hades and explains who he is, and his mission in a song:
Orph.:   Orpheus I am, come from the deeps below,
            To thee, fond man, the plagues of love to show, etc.
                              —*The Mad Lover,* IV, 1.

Venus: Here, here I present am
           Both in my girdle, and my flame;
           Wherein are woven all the powers
           The Graces gave me, or the Hours,
           My nurses once, with all the arts
           Of gaining and of holding hearts:
           And these with, I descend.
           But to your influences first commend
           The vow I go to take
           On earth, for perfect Love and Beauty's sake.[67]

Following Venus' soliloquy there is an allegorical scenic display, which is described and interpreted in a song concluding the masque.   The last part of the song compliments the various members of the royal family, calling each one by name.

Venus' song ended, "and she rising up to go to the Queen, the throne disappears; in place of which, there shooteth up a palm tree with an imperial crown on top; from the roof whereof, lilies and roses twining together and embracing the stem, flourish through the crown, which she in the SONG with the chorus describes:

Grand Chorus:
           Beauty and Love, whose story is mysterial,
           In yonder palm tree, and the crown imperial,
           Do from the rose and lily, so delicious,
           Promise a shade and shall ever be propitious
           To both the kingdoms.   But to Britain's Genius
           The snaky rod and serpents of Cyllenius
           Bring not more peace than these, who so united be
           By Love, as with it earth and heaven delighted be.
           And who this King and Queen would well historify
           Need only speak their names; these them will glorify;
           Mary and Charles, Charles with his Mary named are,
           And all the rest of Loves or princes famed are." [68]

After this they dance their going out.

Some reference has already been made to the use of song in emphasizing the setting.   The song of the Satyrs [69] addressed to the moon gives the audience imaginative scope for supplying time, place, and atmosphere.   Mr. Noble in *Shakespeare's Use of Song* points out that Shakespeare made music take the place

---

[67] *Love's Triumph,* pp. 365, 366.
[68] *Love's Triumph,* p. 366.
[69] Referred to on page 99.

of scenery. In the play *As You Like It,* the song, *Under the greenwood tree* supplies the setting; *Blow, blow, thou winter wind* suggests the time of year, and the weather; *What shall he have that killed the deer,* takes the place of a forest setting; and *It was a lover and his lass . . . That o'er the green cornfields did pass,* are self-explanatory lines.[70]

Jonson employs the same device in his *Song of Night.* The words of the song paint the stage with mystery, drowsiness; while the spirit of Night itself breathes from the chorus.[71]

" Night rises slowly, and takes her chariot bespangled with stars."

" By this time the Night and the Moon being both risen, Night hovering over the place, sung:

> Break, Phant'sie, from thy cave of cloud,
> And spread thy purple wings;
> Now all thy figures are allowed,
> And various shapes of things;
> Create of airy forms a stream,
> It must have blood and naught of phlegm.

This song is frequently praised by collectors of lyric verse.

The songs in *Chloridia* emphasize the fresh, buoyant joy of spring-time. If Inigo Jones left out any details suggestive of spring-time in his designing, the songs must have contributed enough ideas to present a complete setting. The song of the Rivers, Springs and Fountains suggests the spirit of gladness in playing waterfalls, dashing mists, falling spray. This is one of the most beautiful lyric stanzas in the masque. Critics join in praising it for its graceful imagery, its verbal melody, and appealing allusions.

" All which beheld, the NYMPHS, RIVERS, and FOUNTAINS, with the SPRING, sung this rejoicing SONG:

> Run out, all the Floods, in joy with your silver feet,
> And haste to meet the enamoured Spring,

[70] Richmond Noble, *Shakespeare's Use of Song.* Oxford Univ. Press, 1923, p. 19.

[71] *The Vision of Delight,* p. 216. Compare the first stanza of a three-men's song from Campion's *Lord's Masque:*
> Night as well as brightest day hath her delight
> Let us then with mirth and music deck the night.
> Never did glad day such store
> Of joy to night bequeath:
> Her stars then adore,
> Both in heaven and here beneath.

> For whom the warbling Fountains sing
> The story of the flowers, preserved by the Hours
> At Juno's soft command, and Iris' showers
> Sent to quench jealousy and all those powers
> Of Love's rebellious war:
> Whilst Chloris sits a shining star
> To crown and grace our jolly song, made long
> To the notes that we bring, to glad the Spring.[72]

One of the choruses in the *Golden Age* presents a picture of nature impossible to produce on the stage, yet necessary to complete the imagery of the change that was brought about in the masque:

> The very shrub shall balsam sweat,
> And nectar melt the rock with heat,
> Till earth have drunk her fill;
> That she no harmful weed may know,
> Nor barren fern, nor mandrake low,
> Nor mineral to kill." [73]

Imitation of thunder in the masque *Chloridia* lent certain realistic appeal to the atmosphere. A masquer imitating thunder came on the stage, as the sixth performer symbolizing an element of the weather:

" SIXTH ENTRY:

" Thunder, alone, dancing the tunes to a noise, mixed, and imitating thunder." [75]

Dialogue songs performed two functions; one was the humoring of the composers and the other a carrying forward of the plot by means of musical conversation. A long dialogue occurs between Nature and Prometheus in *Mercury Vindicated*, with a chorus interrupting occasionally to sum up or emphasize some particular phase of the action.[76] In the *Golden Age*, Astrea, Pallas, and the Golden Age carry on a three part conversation, with the chorus chiming in to generalize the effect, or emphasize what is most essential to the main theme of the masque.[77]

[72] *Chloridia*, p. 372. Fletcher uses a similar topic in the song Nilus sings:

> Make room for my rich water's fall,
> And bless my flood; . . . etc.
> *The False One*, III, 4.

[73] The *Golden Age Restored*, p. 199.
[75] *Chloridia*, p. 371.
[76] *Mercury Vindicated*, p. 193.
[77] *Golden Age*, p. 197.

Love's Triumph presents a short song in which four characters each contribute one line or more to the main idea of the masque, and a grand chorus finishes off the conclusion:

Song

Jupiter, Juno, Genius, Hymen

Jup.:	Haste, daughter Venus, haste and come away,
Jun.:	All powers that govern marriage, pray
	That you will lend your light,
Gen.:	Unto the constellation of this night.
Hym.:	Hymen.
Jun.:	And Juno.
Gen.:	And the Genius call.
Jup.:	Your father Jupiter
Grand Cho.:	And all
	That bless or honor holy nuptial.[78]

Dialogues from the masques, *For the Honour of Wales*,[79] *Chloridia*,[80] *The Fortunate Isles*,[81] have been quoted elsewhere in this discussion. Further illustrations of the dialogue type of song occur in the *Masque of the Gypsies*,[82] the *Masque of Augurs*,[83] *Time Vindicated*.[84]

An interesting note showing that song might be used to fill in time between dances occurs in the *Masque of Beauty*. Obviously, the dancers were tired, and needed time to rest, or to prepare for the next dance. The poem is frequently included in anthologies and probably deserved the attention focused on it in the masque.

. . . "they danced forth their second dance, more subtle and full of change than the former; and so exquisitely performed, as the king's majesty (incited first by his own liking to that which all others there present wished) required them both again, after some time of dancing with the lords. *Which time, to give them respite, was intermitted with a song;* first by a treble voice, in this manner:

[78] *Love's Triumph*, p. 365.
[79] See p. 107 of this chapter.
[80] See p. 93 of this chapter.
[81] The *Fortunate Isles*, see page 26 of Chapter I.
[82] *Masque of the Gypsies*, p. 271.
[83] *Masque of Augurs*, p. 303.
[84] *Time Vindicated*, pp. 314–315.

> If all these Cupids, now were blind,
> As is their wanton brother:
> Or play should put it in their mind
> To shoot at one another:
> What pretty battle they would make,
> If they their object should mistake
> And each one wound his mother." [85]

Jonson's dependence upon music can not be estimated accurately, from his vague comments. We know that he relied upon music to supplement words and action. There is one indication, already mentioned, in the introduction (page 6), that when his power over words deserted him, he utilized the strains of music to express intangible emotions:

> *Genius:*   . . . "But, O,
> My joys like waves, each other overcome,
> And gladness drowns where it begins to flow!
> Some greater Powers speak out, for mine are dumb!

At this was the place filled with rare and choice Music, to which was heard the following SONG, delivered by an excellent voice, and the burden maintained by the whole Quire."

In addition to the passages already quoted in which deities and supernatural beings were especially dependent upon music for dignity, airy grace, or awe, the witches in the *Masque of Queens* deserve special mention. The actual setting for the witches' songs or incantations has not been identified. Jonson's witches sang to no ordinary accompaniment, but to strange, wild, and grotesque strains. While their conversation was carried on in monotones, there was very likely a differentiation between the

---

[85] Beauty, p. 55. Notes from Alphonso Ferrabosco's *Book of Ayres*, 1609, XVIII. Campion also introduces song to give the masquers time to rest: " The Masquers begin their first new entering dance; after it, while they breathe, the time is entertained with a dialogue song." The *Lord's Masque, op. cit.,* p. 82. The song itself contains the words implying that the dancers were resting:

> Breathe again while we with music
> Fill the empty space, . . . etc.

Campion used the same device in his masque for the marriage of Somerset, and the Lady Frances Howard: The third song of three parts, with a chorus of five parts, sung after the first dance:

> While dancing rests, fit place to music granting,
> Good spells the Fates shall breathe, all envy daunting,
> Kind ears with joy enchanting, chanting.

> *Chorus:* Like looks, like hearts, like loves are linked together.

monotone of conversation and the more song-like incantations.
A singing tone accompanied by odd instruments, distinguished
the witches' monologues from the conversation of mortal masquers.

The winding of the cornet, and playing of pipes in the *Masque
of Oberon* added pastoral charm to the actions of the Satyr.
His part was infinitely more Sylvan, more wild, free, and playful
because of his music.   Apollo sang whenever he had any message
to convey to mortals.   On the other hand, the speeches of ordinary
human beings were usually not set to music.   In the *Masque of
Hymen*, the character, Reason, spoke all of her lines.   Being an
allegorical figure with no claim to aesthetic qualities, Reason
did not depend upon emotional atmosphere.   In *Pan's Anniversary*, the nymphs and echoes sing, but the mortals, a shepherd,
and a fencer speak their lines.   In *Neptune's Triumph*, Apollo
and the deities and superhuman creatures sing, while the cook,
the poet, and the boy speak.

There was usually song incidental to the shifting of scenery.
Music either obliterated the creaking of mechanical devices, or
intensified the effect of a changed background. . . . " after the
music had done which waited on the turning of the machine,
[Fame] called from thence to Heroic Virtue, and spake this following speech." [88]

The Fortunate Isles contains a similar coincidence of scene
changing to musical accompaniment :

" Here the scene opens, and the MASQUERS are discovered sitting in their several sieges.   The air opens above, and Apollo,
with Harmony, and the Spirits of Music, sing, while the island
moves forward." [89]

Music accompanied the retreat of the island as well, " This
sung, the island goes back, whilst the Upper Chorus takes it from
them, and the masquers prepare for their figure." [90]

Chloridia presents an extremely complicated change of scene
including the flight of the goddess, Fame, from earth to heaven :
" Here out of the earth ariseth a hill and on top of it a globe, on
which Fame is seen standing with her trumpet in her hand; and
on the hill are seated four persons, presenting POESY, HISTORY,

[88] *Queens,* p. 127.
[89] *Fortunate Isles,* p. 356.
[90] *Ibid.,* p. 358.

ARCHITECTURE, and SCULPTURE, who, together with the NYMPHS, FLOODS, and FOUNTAINS make a full Quire, at which FAME begins to mount, *and moving her wings flieth singing up to Heaven.*" [91]   (The italics are mine.)

PART IV.   CONCLUDING SONGS

The proper conclusion for a masque was a song, or a dance, or a combination of both.   Perhaps singing was more advantageous from the poet's point of view than dancing, because it gave him a last opportunity to convey definite meanings, which dancing could merely symbolize.   Like the dance, it drew all of the masquers together for a single purpose, and gave them a chance to make a graceful exit.[92]   Jonson used final songs to summarize events, point out allegorical interpretations, and to draw conclusions from the preceding action.

A song left an impression of the general tone of the masque; it gave a definite sensory memory of pomp, power, grandeur for the onlooker to carry away with him.

The conclusion of the *Masque of Blackness* is a song bidding the nymphs to shout with joy.   The final impression is that of hilarity.   It bids the audience share in the feeling of exhilaration and triumph, in the success of the performance.   The words, " back, back " are fittingly applied to the retiring nymphs, as they make their exit:

" At which, in a dance, they returned to sea, where they took their shell, and with this full song went out:

> Now Dian with her burning face,
> Declines apace:
> By which our waters know
> To ebb, that late did flow.
> Back seas, back nymphs; but with a forward grace,

---

[91] *Chloridia,* p. 373.

[92] Samuel Daniel also employed song as a convenient means of getting his characters off the stage: " whereunto the three graces retiring themselves aside, sang; " *Vision of the Twelve Goddesses,* Samuel Daniel, English Masques, *op. cit.,* p. 7.   Shakespeare's use of an exit song has been previously quoted in connection with the song *Jog on, jog on, Winters Tale,* IV, 2.   His *I am gone sir and anon, sir,* served the same purpose.   *Twelfth Night,* IV, Sc. 2.

> Keep still your reverence to the place;
> And shout with joy of favour, you have won,
> In sight of Albion, Neptune's son.[93]

The closing of the *Masque of Queens* is a song praising the triumph of good Fame, and very subtly complimenting the excellent performance of the twelve queens. The song must have left a warm feeling of satisfaction in the hearts of the masquers, as well as a pleasant impression on the audience. The last sentence suggests the traditional fairy story ending,—"and they lived happily ever after." Jonson's concluding songs are particularly noteworthy for the tone of finality each one suggests.

. . . "their return to the House of Fame [was] celebrated with this last Song, whose notes (as the former) were the work and honour of my excellent friend, Alfonso Ferrabosco." [94]

> " Who, Virtue, can thy power forget,
>   That sees these live and triumph yet?
> The Assyrian pomp, the Persian pride,
> Greek's glory; and the Roman's died;
>   And who yet imitate
> Their noises tarry the same fate.
> Force greatness all the glorious ways
> You can, it soon decays:
> But so good Fame shall never;
> Her triumphs, as their causes, are forever." [95]

The last song in the *Masque of Oberon* picks up the action, explains the situation, gives a reason for the vanishing of the star, and like the last of Tennyson's *Idylls,* heralds the approach of a new dawn.

"After this, they danced their last dance into the work. And with a full SONG the star vanished, and the whole machine closed:

> O yet how early, and before her time,
> The envious morning up doth climb,
> Though she not love her bed!
> What haste the jealous sun doth make,
> His fiery horses up to take,
> And once more show his head!
> Lest, taken with the brightness of this night,

[93] *Blackness,* p. 44.
[94] *Queens,* p. 128.
[95] *Queens,* p. 129.

The world should wish it last, and never miss his light." [96]

The concluding songs for *Love Freed,* and *Love Restored,* each complete a theme dealing with rescuing Cupid from an unfortunate situation and placing him in a high position of honor. According to the song from *Love Freed* the sun is about to set and masquers must go to rest. The song from *Love Restored* implies that the masquers are weary, and the whole court will enjoy a rest.

The Bard's song concluding the *Irish Masque* is a compliment to the King, rationalizing his policies toward Ireland, and praising his attitude. The masque on the whole is crude and rough, chiefly composed of coarse dialogue. The last song, however, leaves the audience with an impression of a dignified performance, a song quite in keeping with the theme of the masque and temper of the court.

" During this song, the MASQUERS let fall their mantles, and discover their masquing apparel. Then they dance forth:

Song

So breaks the sun earth's rugged chains,
Wherein rude winter bound her veins;
So grows both stream and source of price,
That lately fettered were with ice.
So naked trees get crisped heads,
And coloured coats the roughest meads,
And all get vigour, youth, and spright,
That are but looked on by his light."

A boisterous rolicking song, in harmony with the tone of the masque, concludes the *Masque of Christmas.*[99]   Christmas pre-

[96] Oberon, p. 155. The closing song of Shirley's *Triumph of Peace* combines two of Jonson's methods of ending masques. The first stanza is a " Come away " (p. 51 of Ch. II) song, and the second stanza proclaims a coming day:

    1. Come away, away, away, etc.
    2. Ye feather footed Hours run
        To dress the chariot of the Sun; etc.

The exit song for Campion's *Lord's Masque* is very brief, but the last lines are very conclusive:

    The cocks already crow:
    Dance then and go!

Campion's masque for the marriage of Somerset and Frances Howard ends with a very effective good-night song:

    Haste abord, hast now away! . . . etc.

[99] *Masque of Christmas,* p. 207.

dicts a continuation of his sport the next year, boasting of his own success at the masquing business, and offering the shopkeepers a share in the revels at some future time.

The *Masque of Lethe* closes with a succinct chorus, which points out and develops the masque theme. The predominant mood is that of care-free love, forgetfulness, insouciance:

" *Cho.:*   All then take cause of joy; for who hath not?
            Old Lethe, that their follies are forgot;
            We that their lives unto their fates they fit;
            They that they still shall love, and love with wit." [100]

A peculiar sort of anti-climax occurs at the close of *Time Vindicated*. Diana is introduced shortly before the final song. To give proper emphasis to the King's favorite sport, Jonson placed the song which honored the hunt in the most important position in the masque. The masque had been drawn out to sufficient length before Diana's introduction, so that it was necessary to conclude as rapidly as possible. The final song pays tribute to Diana as Goddess of the hunt, presents her gracefully, though tardily, and concludes the entire masque.

> *Grand Chorus:*
> Turn hunters, then,[101]
>   Again
> Hunting, it is the noblest exercise,
> Makes men laborious, active, wise,
> Bring health, and doth the spirits delight,
> It helps the hearing and the sight:
> It teacheth arts that never slip
> The memory, good horsemanship,
> Search, sharpless courage and defence,
> And chaseth all ill habits thence
> Turn hunters then,
>   Again,
> But not of men.
> Follow his ample
> And just example,
> That hates all chase of malice and of blood;
> And studies only ways of good,

[100] *Lethe*, p. 214.

[101] Dekker's Hunting Song includes the phrase: " 'tis sport to content a King." The song is the third stanza of a long three-stanza song, beginning with a verse on hay-making. The last stanza begins:

> Winde, jollie Hunts-men, your neat bugles shrilly,
> Hounds make a lusty crie: . . . etc.

To keep soft peace in breath.
Man should not hunt mankind to death,
But strike the enemies of man;
Kill Vices if you can;
They are your wildest beasts,
And when they thickest fall, you make the gods true
        feasts." [102]

The closing group of songs in *Chloridia* [103] is in harmony with
the mood of the masque. The dialogue and chorus interpret the
action, explaining the purpose of the masque; the last lines of the
chorus are a series of compliments to the Goddess of Spring and
Flowers, arranged in order of climax. The effect is that of
building up one extravagant idea after another, more operatic
than dramatic in style. The final lines leave an airy, cloud-like
atmosphere of spring-time, an impression of the general idyllic
quality of the masque.

CONCLUSION

While Jonson's guiding principle in song-writing was his sense
for dramatic value, the success of each song depended upon its
lyrical form. Were it not for the peculiar distinctions of the
song-forms, it would be difficult to know whether the lines were
sung, or spoken. The songs in the masques and the songs in the
plays differ very little. Nano's songs, and Nightingale's ballads
carry forward the plot in about the same way that the songs in
the masques further the narrative. But there was more plot for
Nano and Nightingale to carry, than for any corresponding
masque singer. The masques are simple in theme, and the plot,
no matter how generously apportioned to the songs, is never very
heavy.

When Jonson wrote in his best lyrical vein, he gave fully
as beautiful songs to the plays as to the masques. *Slow, slow,
fresh fount,* and *Queen and Huntress* compare favorably with
Break, Phantasie from your Cave of Cloud, and *Run out, all ye
Floods, in joy with your silver feet.* But on the whole, there are
more good lyrics for singing in the masques than in the plays.

Compared with the other masque writers of his day, Jonson
was supreme, and he owed his supremacy to his power over both
lyrical and dramatic forms. Had he possessed ability to compose music, and write songs spontaneously, he might have been

[102] *Time Vindicated,* p. 319.
[103] *Chloridia,* pp. 373, 374.

another Campion, neglecting the principles of dramatic fitness. Campion's masques are all song. They resemble a program of music, rather than a form of dramatic spectacle. The *Masque for the Marriage of Lord Hayes* has scarcely a speech; and the other masques obviously depend for their appeal upon musical effects. Campion's masques contain minute descriptions of the instruments used, the effect produced by playing on them, and the appeal of various vocal harmonies. But his songs, beautiful as they are from a purely lyric point of view, were probably not as effective when produced as Jonson's. They lacked the dramatic intensity for which Jonson so carefully schemed and plotted.

As songs, Campion's separate compositions far surpassed those of any other masque writer. He made up his own melodies, and felt no restrictions. He could even write long songs, if he chose, such as a poet would not have dared to present to a composer. He used irregular line-lengths if the spirit moved him. His repetitions are written out rather than indicated, and his variety of subject matter unlimited. His euphonious effects are the result of spontaneous emotion, not of artful arrangement. Lacking speeches, Campion used expository, argumentative, narrative, or descriptive matter for his themes; and he handled his subject matter with such skill that he turned ill chosen material into melodic verse. Campion was something of a freak as a masque writer; his masques are an expression of exceptional lyric power. Daniel was akin to Campion, in depending upon musical effects for appeal, yet Daniel was not a master of music and his songs are not so successful as Campion's. He lacked Campion's power over melody, and Jonson's dramatic sense.

Swinging to the opposite extreme from Campion, Peele and Webster wrote masques depending upon dramatic effects, and lacking songs. Chapman, more than any other writer, arranged his songs in the fashion of Jonson. His sense of balancing dramatic effect, and lyric forms was not as acute as Jonson's, and his masques were less successful. Chapman tended to write better singing songs, but arranged them with less care for their dramatic fitness. His entertainments proved to be lacking in dramatic color. Davenant followed Chapman, several steps in the rear. If Chapman lacked color, Davenant lacked character. His songs have neither lyric beauty, nor dramatic fitness.

Davenant's sense of balance between the two was fairly enough drawn, but intensity of feeling was lacking. His masques are weak smatterings, compared with Jonson's vital structures.

Carew's masque partook of the nature of Campion's and Davenant's. He depended upon lyrical appeal to such an extent that his masque turned out to be lifeless. Middleton's masque differs from Carew's in having much vigor, with dramatic rather than lyric power; but his work is not particularly outstanding among the masques of his day.

Shirley and Townsend followed Jonson's masque forms, so far as they were able. They strained for dramatic effect, but strained too hard, and their efforts resulted in the employment of tricks and mechanical devices. They depended upon pageantry and spectacle more than Jonson did. Their songs likewise strained for effect. They used odd musical instruments to attract attention, and cared more for outlandish bird calls than for the tone-shading of euphonious song. Their masques are pageants, their songs lack restraint and melody, their dramatic effects lack force.

Jonson's pathway as a masque writer led him in and out between extremes of all kinds. At times he wavered to the right or the left, but never far enough to endanger his progress. He could not have touched Campion, and he would not have lingered long with Middleton and Peele. He paid no heed to the others, for they were but aberrations of his shadow. Had he met Milton, who knows where he might have wandered, who knows where he might have dwelt?

Granting that Jonson was supreme in the field of masque writing, supreme with the exception, possibly, of Milton, it is difficult even by processes of comparing and contrasting his masques with those of other writers, to appreciate fully Jonson's understanding of masque problems. It should have been simple enough for any poet to write lyrical speeches. It was not difficult for men of small ability to make suggestions as to stage settings, or the character of the dances. But to plan a well balanced design and to plan in advance the dramatic effects of a singer's pitch, or volume, or the timbre of an instrument—this required something beyond mere facility with words.

Jonson's contemporaries knew him as a playwright, as a literary dictator and wit, as a writer of court masques. Dazzled by his learning, by his friendship with the King, by his prolific writings of plays and poems, they were proud to imitate his style.   They thought it an honor to be counted among his sons.   Some of them may have been more musically gifted than Jonson himself; Herrick addressed verses to his lute which reveal an intimate knowledge of the instrument.   Field and Brome wrote songs for the stage.   Randolph, Vaughn, Woodard, Crashaw and others made allusions to music which showed them conversant with the technic of the art.   But the music to which they referred was the music of Elizabethan England; and the songs which they wrote were songs for polyphonic settings, for madrigal singing, or airs for the lute.

The fact that this later generation lived during the period of the decline of English music, when the Puritans attempted to restrict the use of music in the churches and in all public places, did not change their ideals of song-form.   The music which these poets heard was Puritan Psalm chanting, or a few arias smuggled in from Italy; but the music which they idealized, which they remembered when they wrote songs, was the music of Byrd, Weelkes, Youll, and Ferrabosco.

The sons of Ben perpetuated in their verse the song-forms of Elizabethan England.   Only a detailed study of the songs of the seventeenth century, songs written during Puritan ascendancy, songs written in Elizabethan form, though they were never intended to be sung, can show how far the influence of Rare Ben Jonson penetrated into future generations.   It is yet to be discovered how much Shelley, Keats, Browning, and even Rupert Brooke may owe to the prestige which Ben Jonson conferred upon the song-form of the Elizabethan composers.

BIBLIOGRAPHY

Manuscripts Containing the Music for Jonson's Songs

Ferrabosco, Alphonso. "Gay Kind Fairy," Coranto from Love's Triumph. Brit. Mus. ms. 34204.

Ferrabosco, Alphonso. "Beauties Have ye seen this toy?" from The Hue and Cry after Cupid. Brit. Mus. ms. Add. 116048.

Anonymous. "Drink to me only with thine eyes." Brit. Mus. ms. 29386 fol. 12b.

Anonymous. "Have you seen but a bright lily grow?" in two mss. Add. 11518 and 34204.

Anonymous. "If I freely may discover," Poetaster, II, 1. Brit. Mus. ms. 24665.

Stevens, R. J. S. Witches Songs from the Masque of Queens. 18th Cent. Brit. Mus. ms. Add. 31815. (Feb. 1, 1895.)

Manuscripts of Other Music Useful in Preparing This Study, Chiefly Ferraboscan Music

Madrigals by Ferrabosco. Brit. Mus. ms. 31414.

Thirteen Fantasies by Ferrabosco. Brit. Mus. ms. Add. 29427 ff46b–52b.

Collection of Songs by Ferrabosco. Brit. Mus. ms. Add. 32377 f. 4.

Another Collection of Songs by Ferrabosco. Brit. Mus. ms. 31, 392 ff 13b–38.

Short Pieces for the Lute including a Galliarde. ms. Harl. 7578 ff118–23.

Fancies by Ferrabosco. Brit. Mus. ms. Add. 32377f (5b–25b).

A Treatise on Dauncinge. Brit. Mus. ms. Sl. 904 fol. 135.

Directions to Daunce Several Daunces. ms. Harl. 364.

Lawes, Henry. Five Songs from Comus. Brit. Mus. ms. 11518.

Lawes, Henry. Masques and Tunes. Brit. Mus. ms. 10444; 10445.

Directions for playing the flute and examples of all the flats and sharps. Brit. Mus ms. 34204 (Add.).

Chamber Music of the Seventeenth Century containing lute music by Alphonso Ferrabosco. Brit. Mus. ms. Add. 31423.

Early Printed Song-Books Containing Music for Jonson's Words

Youll, Henry. *Canzonets for Three Voyces*, 1608.

Ferrabosco, Alphonso. *Book of Ayres*, 1609.

Peerson, Martin. *Private Music*, 1620.

Playford, John. *Select Ayres and Dialogues*, 1653; 1669.

Miscellaneous

Adams, J. Q. *Dramatic Records of Sir Henry Herbert, Master of the Revels*, Yale Univ. Press, New Haven, 1917.

Adams, J. Q. and Bradley, J. F. *Jonson Allusion Book*, New Haven, Yale Univ. Press, 1922.

Albright, V. E. *The Shakespearean Stage,* 1909, Columbia Press, New York.

Alden, Raymond M. *An Introduction to Poetry,* New York, Henry Holt and Co., 1909.

Anderson, H. Orsmond. *Early English Music, Musical Opinion,* London, 1920.

Antcliff, Herbert. *The Affinity of Music and Literature,* from the *Monthly Musical Record,* London, 1906.

Arber, R. *English Garner* (Ed. Sydney Lee) 1879–83. 8 Vols.

Arkwright, G. E. P. *Studies in Music,* Scribners, 1901. Robin Grey's *Studies in Music,* pp. 199–214, contains an article on the Ferrabosco Family.

Aubrey, John. *Brief Lives,* ed. Andrew Clark, Oxford at the Clarendon Press, 1898.

Ault, Norman. *Elizabethan Lyrics from Original Texts,* Longmans, Green and Co., New York, 1925. *Seventeenth Century Lyrics,* Longmans, Green and Co., New York, 1928.

Bacon, Francis. *Syva Sylvarum,* printed for W. Lee, London, 1631.

Baskerville, Charles Reade. *English Elements in Jonson's Early Comedies,* Univ. of Texas Pub., Austin, Texas, 1911.

Baskerville, Charles Reade. *Sources of Jonson's Masque of Christmas and Lovers Made Welcome,* Mod. Philol., Vol. 6, 1903.

Bayly, Anselm. *Alliance of Poetry and Music and Oratory,* (Paradise Lost), London, 1789.

Beaumont and Fletcher. Works, ed. A. Glover and A. R. Waller, 10 vol., 1905–12.

Blomfield, R. T. Inigo Jones, Portfolio, 1889.

Boughton, Rutland. *Shakespeare's Ariel,* A Study of Musical Character, *Musical Quarterly,* New York, 1916, Vol. II, No. 4.

Bridges, Frederick. *Shakespearean Music in the Plays and Early Operas,* New York, G. P. Dutton and Co., 1923.

Bridges, Frederick. *Songs from Shakespeare,* Novello and Co., London, 1926.

British, The Minstrel, Vol. I, Glasgow, 1843.

Briggs, William Dinsmore. *Studies in Ben Jonson, Anglia,* Vol. 39, 1914.

Brotanek, Rudolph. *Die Englischen Maskenspiele,* Englischen Philologie, Vol. XV, Leipsig, Germany.

Brome, Richard. *Dramatic Works of,* published by John Pearson, York Street Covent Garden, London, 1873, in three volumes.

Brown, James A. *Music and British Authors, Monthly Musical Record,* London, 1909.

Bullen, A. H. *Lyrics from Elizabethan Dramatists,* London, 1888.

Bullen, A. H. *Lyrics from the Old Song-Books,* London, Lawrence and Bullen, 1897.

Bullen, A. H. *More Lyrics from the Song Books of the Elizabethan Age,* London, 1888.

Bullen, A. H. *Shorter Elizabethan Poems,* Westminster, Archibald Constable and Co. Ltd., 1903.

Burney, Dr. Chas. *A General History of Music,* London, 1789. 4 vols.

Byrd, William. Psalms and Sonnets, 1588. Songs of Sundry Natures, 1589, 1610. Second Book of Songs, 1611.

Calendar of State Papers, Domestic Series, of the Reign of James I, 1603–10, ed. Mary Anne Everette Green, London, 1857.

Cambridge History of English Literature, see Volume VI on *Masques* and also *Ben Jonson.*

Campbell, Lily B. *Scenes and Machines on the English Stage.* Cambridge Univ. Press, 1923.

Campion, Thomas, *Poetical Works of,* ed. Percival Vivian, New York, E. P. Dutton and Co.

Campion, Thomas. *The Works of Thomas Campion,* ed. by A. H. Bullen, Chiswick Press, London, 1889.

Carpenter, F. I. *English Poetry,* 1500–1700, London, 1897.

Carpenter, F. I. *Outline Guide to the Study of English Lyric Poetry,* 1897.

Cartwright, William. Life and Poems of, ed. C. Goffin. Cambridge Univ. Press, 1918.

Castelaine, M. *Ben Jonson,* Paris, 1909.

Catches, Rounds, and Canons, printed for John Hilton, London, 1652. Ed. Bullen, London, 1906. Notes on Hist.

Chambers, E. K. Accounts of the Revels Office; and *The English Stage.* Oxford Clarendon Press, 1923.

Chappell, William. *Popular Music in the Olden Time* in 2 volumes, Cramer, Beale and Chappell, 201, Regent Street, London.

Collier, J. P. *The Annals of the Stage to the Restoration,* 3 vols., 1831. Seven English Poetical Miscellanies, London, 1867.

Cowling, G. H. *Music on the Shakespearean Stage,* Cambridge Univ. Press, 1913.

Cox, F. A. *English Madrigalists in the time of Shakespeare,* London, J. M. Dent and Co., 1899.

Cunliffe, John W. *Italian Prototypes of the Masque and Dumb Show,* Mod. Lang. Assoc., Vol. 22, 1909.

Cunliffe, J. W. *The Masque in Shakespeare's Plays.*

Dabney, J. P. *The Musical Basis of Verse,* New York, Longmans, Green and Co., 1901.

Daniel, Samuel, *Complete Works of,* in 5 vols. Ed. A. B. Grossart, London, 1885.

Davenant, William, *Dramatic Works of.* Ed. H. Sothern and Co., London, 1874.

Davey, Henry. *History of English Music,* London, J. Curwen and Sons, 1921, 2 vols.

Davison, Francis. *Poetical Rhapsody,* 1602; 1611; 1621; repr. Bullen, 1890, in 2 vols.

Dekker, Thomas, *Dramatic Works of,* in 4 vols. Ed. John Pearson, London, 1873.

Dekkar, Thomas, the *Plague Pamphlets of.* Ed. E. P. Wilson, Oxford Clarendon Press, 1925.

Dickinson, Edward. *The Study of the History of Music,* New York, Chas. Scribner and Sons, 1920.

Dickinson, Helen and Clarence. *Excursions in Musical History,* New York, Knickerbocker Press, 1917.

Donne, John, *Poems of.* Ed. H. J. C. Grierson, The Clarendon Press, Oxford, 1912.

Donne, John. *A Study in Discord,* see Fausset.

Drayton, Michael, *Complete Works of.* Ed. J. R. Smith, London, 1876.

Drayton, Michael, *A Critical Study of Michael Drayton,* by Oliver Eltin, London, 1905.

Drummond, William, *Poems of.* Edited by James Stilke, Edinburgh, 1852.

Drummond, William, *Notes of Ben Jonson's Conversation with.* Printed for the Shakes. Soc., London, 1842.

Du Bois, Abbe. *Critical Reflections on Poetry, Painting, and Music,* London, 1748.

Duncan, Edmonstoune. *The Story of Minstrelsy,* New York, 1907.

Duncan, Edmonstoune, *Lyrics from the Old Song Books,* Harcourt, Brace and Co., New York, 1927.

Dunn, Esther C. *Ben Jonson's Art,* Smith College, Northampton, Mass., 1925.

Elson, Arthur. *Literary Errors about Music, Mus. Quarterly,* New York, 1917.

Elson, Louis C. *Shakespeare in Music,* Boston, L. C. Page and Co. 1901.

English Music 1604–1904, Music Story Series. Ed. Frank. J. Crowest.

Erasmus, Desiderus. *Epistolae,* Oxford Press, London, 1906. Ed. Henry Frowde.

Erskine, John. *Elizabethan Lyric,* MacMillan and Co. New York, 1903.

Evans, H. A. *English Masques,* London, 1897

Evans, Edwin. *Analogues and Associations of Music and Literature,* Transactions of the Royal Soc. of Literature, London, 1914.

Fausset, Hugh I., *John Donne, a Study in Discord,* London, 1924.

Fellowes, Edmund Horace. *English Madrigal Composers,* Oxford, Clarendon Press, 1921.

Fellowes, E. H. *English Madrigal Verse.* Clarendon Press, Oxford.

Fellowes, E. H. *The English Madrigal,* Oxford University Press, London, 1925.

Fellowes, E. H. *The English Madrigal School,* A series of Song-books . . . Stainer and Bell, London, 1913. *William Byrd,* Oxford at the Clarendon Press, 1923.

Feuillerat, A. *John Lyly,* Rennes, 1910.

Feuillerat, A. Documents Relating to the Office of the Revels in the Time of Queen Elizabeth. Louvain, 1908.

Ferrabosco, Alphonso. *Book of Ayres,* 1609.

Ferrabosco, Alphonso. *Songs for the Viol,* 1609.

Ferrabosco, *The Family of the Ferraboscos,* an article by Giovanni Livi, *Musical Antiquary,* London, 1913, V. 4, No. 15.

Ferrabosco, Alphonso, an article in *Robin Grey's Studies,* see Arkwright, G.

Ferrabosco, Alphonso, see Manuscripts listed.

Fleay, F. G. *A Biographical Chronicle of the English Drama, 1559–1642*, 1891, London, 2 vols.

Flood, W. H. G. *A New Light on Early Tudor Composers*, Mus. Times, No. 921, Vol. 60.

Förster, Max. "Shakespeare—Musik," *Germanisch-Romanische Monatsschrift*, XVI, 1928, pp. 298–304.

Ford, John. *The Dramatic Works of Massinger and Ford*, Introduc. by Hartley Coleridge, London, 1839.

Furnivall, F. J. A List of all the Songs and Passages in Shakespeare which have been set to Music. Compiled by J. Greenhill, W. A. Harrison, and F. J. Furnivall, London, New Shakes. Soc., 1884.

Galpin, F. W. *Old English Instruments of Music*, London, Methuen and Co., 1910.

Gildersleeve, V. *Government Regulation of the Elizabethan Theater*, 1908.

Gosson, Stephen. *Short Apologie for the School of Abuse*, 1587.

Graves, T. S. (Court Theaters.) Court and London Theaters during the Reign of Eliz., 1913.

Greg, Walter Wilson, *A list of Masques, Pageants, etc.*, printed for the Bibliographical Soc. of London, 1902.

Groves. *Dictionary of Music and Musicians*. Ed. H. C. Coles. 5 vols. London, Macmillan and Co., 1927.

Harding, H. A. *The Alliance of Music and Poetry*, Mus. Standard, London, 1917.

Harris, Clement A. *Musical Allusions of Great Writers*, Mus. Quarterly, N. Y., 1916.

Hathaway, Chas. Montgomery. *The Alchemist*, Yale Studies, 1903.

Harvey, Gabriel. *Letter Book*. Ed. John Scott. Printed for the Camden Soc., 1884.

Harvey, Gabriel. *Marginalia*, Shakespeare Head Press, Stratford upon Avon, 1913.

Hawkins, Sir John. (History of Music.) *A General History of the Science and Practice of Music*, London, T. Payne and Son, 1776, 5 vol.

Henslowe's *Diary*. Ed. W. W Greg, London, 1904

Hepple, Norman *Lyrical Forms in English Verse*, Cambridge Univ. Press, 1916.

Herrick, Robert. *Poetical Works*, ed. F. W. Moorman, London, Milford, 1921.

Heseltine, Philip, see Warlock, Philip.

Heywood, Thomas. *Dramatic Works of*, edited by Pearson, in 6 vols. 1874.

Hilton, John, see *Catches*.

Holiday, Barten. *Technogomania*, 1618, 1630. The songs quoted are included also in Bliss Reed's *Songs from the Brit. Drama*.

Holinshed's *Chronicles of England, Scotland and Ireland*, 1577–1586-7; reprinted 1807–8, 6 vols.

Hull, A. E. *Shakespeare and Music*, Monthly Mus. Record, London, 1916.

Hume, M. A. *Courtships of Queen Elizabeth*, London, 1896.

Hunt, Mary Leland. *Thomas Dekkar,* Columbia Dissertation, New York, 1911.

Jones, Robert. Book of Songs, 1601; First Set of Madrigals, 1607; Ultimum Vale, 1608; A Musical Dream, 1609; Muses Garden of Delights, 1610. Reprinted and published W. B. Squire, 1901.

Jones, Inigo, *Designs by,* ed. by Percy Simpson for the Walpole Society, 1923–24. *Engravings from the Masques.*

Jonson, Ben. *Works.* Ed. William Gifford in 9 vols., 1816. Ed. Cunningham and Gifford in 1875, 9 vols. Mermaid Edition, 3 vols., ed. Nicholson and Herford, Unwin, London, 1893–95. Complete Works, ed. Simpson and Herford, 1925, 3 vols. in progress.

Jonson, Ben, *Songs of.* Edited by E. and L. Pisaro, Limited to 175 paper and 10 vellum copies, Eragny Press, The Brook, Hammersmith, London, 1906.

Jusserand, J. J. *A Literary History,* G. P. Putnam and Sons, New York, 1895–1900.

Krehbiel, H. E. *English Virginal Music,* Mus. Record and Review, Boston, 1902, No. 492.

Kimmins, G. T. *Songs from the Plays of Shakespeare,* London, Novello and Co., 1911.

Lang, Andrew. *Elizabethan Songs,* Boston, 1894.

Lanier, Sydney. *Shakespeare and His Forerunners,* see Chapter on Music, New York, Doubleday, Page and Co., 1908.

Lanier, Sydney. *The Science of English Verse,* Chas. Scribner's Sons, New York, 1880.

Lawes, Henry, see Lawes, under Manuscripts.

Lawrence, W. J. *The Elizabethan Playhouse and Other Studies,* see Chapter IV on Music in the Elizabethan Theater, J. B. Lippincott and Co., Philadelphia, 1918.

Lawrence, W. J. *Music in the Elizabethan Theater,* Berlin, 1908.

Lodge, Thomas. *Works,* ed. Gosse, Hunterian Club, 1872–82.

Lindsey, Edwin S. *The Music of the Songs in Fletcher's Plays,* Studies in Philol., XXI, April, 1924.

Lindsey, E. S. *The Music in Ben Jonson's Plays,* Modern Language Notes, Vol. XLIV.

Livi, Giovanni. See Ferrabosco.

Lyly, John. *Works,* ed. Bond, 3 vols., 1902.

Lyly, John. See Feuillerat.

Lyrical Miscellanies: Tottel's Miscellany, 1557–1587, reprinted in Arber, 1870; Paradise of Dainty Devices, ed. Edwards, 1576, 8 editions, Brydges, 1810; Gorgeous Gallery, 1578, Helliconia, 1815; Handful of Pleasant Delights; Phoenix Nest, 1593; England's Helicon, 1600–1614; Poetical Rhapsody, Francis Davison, 1602; Seven English Miscellanies, 1867 (this includes all of the above except a Handful of Pleas. delights). Ed. Collier.

Marston, John, *Works,* ed. Bullen, 1887, 3 vols.

Marcham, Frank. *The King's Office of the Revels,* 1610–22, London, 1925.

McDonough, Thomas. *Thomas Campion and the Art of English Poetry,* Dublin, Talbot Press, 1912.

Massinger, Phillip. See John Ford.

Middleton, Thomas, *Works,* ed. Bullen, 1885, 8 vols.

Milton, John, *Complete Poetical Works of,* New York, Houghton Mifflin Co., 1889.

Morely, Thomas. *A Plaine and Easie Introduction to Practickal Musicke,* 1597.

Morely, Thomas. *Triumphs of Orianna,* 1601, pub. in score by Wm. Hawes, London, 1815; Canzonets, 1593; Madrigals to Four Voyces, 1594; Ballets to Five Voyces, 1595.

Morley, Henry. *Masques and Entertainments by Ben Jonson.* See preface, London, 1890.

Munday, Anthony. *John a Kent,* pr. Shakes. Soc. 1851.

Murray, J. T. *English Dramatic Companies,* 1910, 2 vols.

Nabbes, Thomas, *Microsmus.* (In Dodsley's Collection.) *Old Plays,* 1780, Vol. 9, Hannibal and Scipio, London, 1635, 1637.

Naylor, E. W. *Shakespeare and Music,* London, 1896.

Nichols, James. *Progresses and Public Processions of Queen Elizabeth,* 4 vols., 1823; *Progresses, Processions and Magnificent Festivities of James I,* 1828, 4 vols.

Niecks, Frederick. *Instrumental Music in Shakespeare's Day,* Monthly Musical Record, London, 1916.

Noble, Richmond. *Shakespeare's Use of Song,* Oxford, at the Univ. Press, 1916.

Oliphant, Thomas. *Musa Madrigalesca,* Calkins and Budd, London, 1837.

Onions, T. C. *Shakespeare and Music* (Collection of Essays, *Shakespeare's England*), Oxford, Clarendon Press, 1916.

Oxford History of Music, Volumes I and II, ed. Henry Frowde, Oxford, 1901.

Padelford, F. M. *Old English Musical Terms,* Yale Univ. Press, New Haven, 1899.

Palmer, W. H. *Two Thousand Questions and Answers on Musical History, Biography, and Kindred Subjects,* Bristol, W. Crofton Hemmons, 1900.

Patterson, C. B. *The Rhythm of Prose. The Rhythm of Life,* New York, Thomas Cowell and Company, 1915.

Parry, Hubert C. *English Lyrics,* Seventh Set, London, Novello and Co., 1907.

Peacham, Henry. *Compleat Gentleman,* Oxford, 1906. Originally published in 1634.

Peele, George. Coll. *Works,* ed. Bullen, 1882, 2 vols.

Peerson, Martin. Private Music, see Old Books Containing Jonson's Music.

Pell Records, for the Reign of James I. Issues of the Exchequer, London, 1836.

Pepys, Samuel, *Diary,* E. P. Dutton and Co., New York, 1908.

Playford, John. *Select Ayres and Dialogues,* 1653, 1669.

Potter, Frank Hunter. *Reliquarry of English Song,* G. Schirmer and Co., New York, 1915.

Pound, Louise, *The Ballad and the Dance,* Mod. Lang. Assoc., Vol. 24, 1919.

Pulver, Jeffrey. *The Music of Ben Jonson,* Monthly Musical Record, Feb., Mar., 1923.

Pulver, Jeffrey. *Music in England During the First Half of the Sixteenth Century,* Mus. Times, London, 1919, Vol. 60.

Pulver, Jeffrey. *A Dictionary of Old English Music and Musical Instruments,* E. P. Dutton and Co., New York, 1923.

Pulver, Jeffrey. *A Biographical Dictionary of Old English Music,* E. P. Dutton and Co., New York, 1927.

Quarry, W. E. *A Dictionary of Musical Compositions and Composers,* E. P. Dutton and Co., New York.

Randolph, Thomas, *The Poems and Amyntas of,* ed. J. J. Parry, New Haven, Yale Univ. Press, 1917.

Rashdall, Hastings. *Universities of Europe in the Middle Ages,* Oxford at the Clarendon Press, 2 volumes, 1905.

Reed, Edward Bliss. *English Lyrical Poetry,* New Haven, Yale Univ. Press, 1912; *Songs from the British Dramatists,* New Haven, Yale Univ. Press, 1925.

Renwick, W. L. *Edmund Spenser,* London, 1925.

Rehyer, Paul. *Les Masques Anglais,* Paris, 1909.

Rimbault, E. F., ed., *The Old Cheque Book of the Chapel Royal,* Camden Soc., 1872.

Rhys, Ernest. *Lyric Poetry,* London, J. M. Dent and Sons, 1913.

Ritson, J. *Select Collection of English Songs,* London, 1813.

Rowley, Samuel. *The Noble Soldier,* London, 1634.

Saintsbury, George. *A History of Elizabethan Literature,* MacMillan and Co., New York, 1887.

Schelling, Felix E. *English Literature During the Lifetime of Shakespeare,* Henry Holt and Co., revised edition, 1927.

Schelling, F. E. *Ben Jonson and the Classical School,* Mod. Lang. Assoc. 1998, Vol. XXII, XIII.

Schelling, F. E. *Elizabethan Drama,* New York, Houghton Mifflin Co., 1908.

Schelling, F. E. *A Book of Elizabethan Lyrics,* Boston, Ginn and Co., 1895.

Scholes, P. A. *The Purpose of Shakespeare's Music,* Proceedings of the Musical Assoc., London, 1917.

Sear, H. G. *Shakespeare and the Orchestra,* Musical Standard, London, 1921.

Sears, Minnie Earl. See *Song Index.*

Shakespeare, William. *All the Songs and Passages of Shakespeare Set to Music,* see Furnivall.

Shakespeare, William. Complete Works, Houghton Mifflin Co., New York, 1906.

Shakespeare, William. Instrumental Music, see Niecks, F. Instrumental Music in Shakespeare's Day, Monthly Mus. Record, London, 1916.

Shakespeare, Musician, see Welch, R. D. (Mus. Quart., New York, 1922).

Shakespeare and Music, see Elson, Naylor, Noble, etc.

Shirley, James. *Dramatic Works,* with Notes by William Gifford, London, 1833.

Simpson, Percy. See *Ben Jonson, The Man and His Work,* ed. Herford and Simpson, see *Engravings from the Masques,* Walpole Soc.

Small, R. A. *The Stage Quarrel between Ben Jonson and the So-called Poetasters,* Breslau, 1899.

Smith, George Gregory. *Ben Jonson,* Macmillan Co., 1919; *Elizabethan Critical Essays,* Oxford at the Clarendon Press, 1904.

Smith, J. Stafford. *Musical Antiqua,* London, 1812–1855.

Song Index, ed. Minnie Earle Sears, New York, H. W. Wilson Co., 1926.

Spaeth, Sigmund G. *Milton's Knowledge of Music,* Princeton, 1913.

Squire, Barclay. See *Shakespeare's England,* Volume II, *Music,* see Robert Jones, also.

Steele, Robert. *The Earliest English Music Printing,* The Bibliographical Soc., London, 1903.

Steele, M. S. *The Plays and Masques at Court, 1558–1642,* New Haven, Yale Univ. Press, 1926.

Stevens, R. J. S. See list of Mss. for the Witches' Songs.

Stopes, C. C. *William Hunnis and the Chapel Royal,* Sh. Jahrbuch XXVII, repr. 1892.

Stowe, John. *A Survey of London,* 1598.

Stubbes, Phillip. *The Anatomy of Abuses,* Repri. Shakes. Soc., 1877, 1882.

Suckling, Sir John, *The Works of,* ed. A. Hamilton Thompson, New York, E. P. Dutton and Co., 1910.

Sullivan, Mary. *Court Masques of James I,* New York, Putnam and Sons Co., 1913.

Swinburne, Chas. A. *A Study of Ben Jonson,* London, 1889.

Symonds, John Addington, *Ben Jonson,* New York, D. Appleton and Co., 1886.

Thorndike, A. H. *Influences of the Court Masque on the Drama,* Mod. Lang. Assoc., Vol. XV, 1900, see also the Chapters on Court Theaters in *Shakespeare's Theater,* New York, MacMillan Co., 1925. See also *Ben Jonson* in the *Cambridge History of English Literature,* Volume VI, Chapter I.

Tudor Church Music, Oxford Press, 1912.

Vincent, C. J. *Fifty Shakespearean Songs,* ed. by Vincent, Boston, Oliver Ditson and Co., 1906.

Walcott, M. E. C. *Memorials of Westminster,* London, 1851.

Walker, E. *History of Music in England,* Vol. III, Oxford, 1907.

Wallace, C. W. *Evolution of the English Drama,* 1912, Berlin, 1912.

Wallace, C. W. The Children of the Chapel of Blackfriars, Univ. Neb. Studies, 1908 (Frieberg, 1906).

Walton, Isaac. Complete Angler, Dutton, New York, 1906. Lives of Dr. John Donne, etc., ed. E. C. Dick, London, 1899.

Warlock, Peter. *The English Ayr,* London, Oxford Univ. Press, 1926,

Warmer, Buck (Ferry and Fellowes), Ramsen, etc., editors of *Tudor Church Music.*

Warner, S. T. *Madrigalists and Lutenists,* Mus. Times, London, Vol. 63, pp. 160–234.

Warren, Joseph. Index to Warren Glees, Catches, Canons, Madrigals, etc., London, 1836.

Weelkes, Thomas. Madrigals, 1577; 1600; Ballets and Madrigals, 1598; 1608; Madrigals for Viols and Voyces, 1600; Airs for Fantastic Sprites, 1608.

Welsford, Enid. *The Court Masque,* Cambridge at the University Press, 1927.

Welch, Christopher. *Six Lectures on the Recorder,* Oxford, 1911.

Wilbye, John. *Two sets of Madrigals:* 1598; 1608.

Wilson, Christopher. *Shakespeare and Music,* London, "The Stage," 1922.

Wilson, Dr. John. *Cheerful Ayres and Ballads,* Oxford, 1660.

Wood, Anthony. Athenae Oxonienses, London, 1813–20, ed. Philip Bliss.

Young Nicholas. *Musica Transalpina,* 1588.

Youll, Henry. *Canzonets,* see early printed books containing music for Ben Jonson's Songs.

Zwager, Nicholas. *Glimpses of Ben Jonson's London,* Swets and Zeitlinger, Amsterdam, 1926.

WESTMAR COLLEGE LIBRARY